Mandarin
phrasebook

Chris Taylor

Mandarin phrasebook
   3rd edition

Published by
   Lonely Planet Publications
   Head Office: PO Box 617, Hawthorn, Vic 3122, Australia
   Branches: 150 Linden Street, Oakland CA 94607, USA
                  10a Spring Place, London NW5 3BH, UK
                  1 rue de Dahomey, 75011 Paris, France

Printed by
   Colorcraft Ltd, Hong Kong

Cover Photograph
   Dazu rock carvings, Sichuan Province

Published
   June1996

National Library of Australia Cataloguing in Publication Data

Taylor, Chris, 1961–
   Mandarin phrasebook.

   3rd ed.
   Includes index.
   ISBN 0 86442 344 6

   1. Chinese language – Conversation and phrase books – English. I. Taylor,Chris,
   1961–. Chinese phrasebook II. Title. III. Title: Chinese phasebook (Series:
   Lonely Planet language survival kit).

495.183421

Contents

From the Publisher

This edition was written by Chris Taylor with assistance from Felicia Zhang and Hsu Shumei. Sally Steward and Louise Callan edited the book. Ann Jeffree was responsible for illustrations, and Penelope Richardson for design. Simon Bracken designed the front cover.

About the Author

Chris Taylor's various occupations have taken him to Australia, London and Tokyo, in between bouts of travel in Asia. He has a degree in English Literature and Mandarin and is the co-author of Lonely Planet's *China* guidebook.

Acknowledgements

Many thanks to Charles and Kate from Chin Communications, and to Kam Y Lau, for their assistance with extra pinyin and script. Thanks to Dan Levin for assisting with the pinyin typesetting.

Introduction

序

Mandarin, as spoken in Beijing, is one of the five major Chinese dialects. It is the official language of the People's Republic of China and is one of the official languages of Singapore. Around 70% of the population in China speaks Mandarin. This doesn't mean that it is their first language, however. In the countryside, people are more likely to speak a local dialect to each other.

The five major dialects subdivide into many more dialects and few of them are mutually intelligible. Chinese, then, is not a language but a family of closely related languages. In mainland China alone there are 1.2 billion Chinese speakers, in Taiwan 20 million and throughout the rest of the world there are large Chinese-speaking communities.

Throughout Chinese history and up to the present, the Chinese grew up speaking the dialect of the region in which they were born. If they learned to read and write, they learned a classical form of the language that was not specific to any regional dialect.

INTRODUCTION

The role of classical Chinese might be compared to that of Latin in Medieval Europe. In the 20th century the Chinese set themselves the task of establishing the dialect of Beijing as a national language. At the same time great effort was put into replacing the archaic written language with a more colloquial one that corresponded more or less to Beijing dialect, or Mandarin as it's known in the West. The result is that today it is possible to use Mandarin throughout China and Taiwan, although the influence of local dialects means that you have to be prepared for some marked differences in regional accents.

If you carry a phrasebook with you in China you will find plenty of opportunities to use it. Although in the big cities there are always a few students around who are keen to practise their English, you'll also find yourself in plenty of situations where there's no-one who has any English. If no-one understands what you're reading from the book, simply point to the Chinese script on the righthand side of the page.

This phrasebook is intended to accompany Lonely Planet's *China* guidebook and the *Cantonese* phrasebook. Used together these books will make your travels in China a lot easier.

Pronunciation

发音

The learner of Chinese encounters the same problem confronting the learner of English: namely the enormous differences in pronunciation that occur from region to region. Consider the bewilderment of the Chinese student of English who travels from Glasgow to New York, or from Sydney to Manchester, and you have some idea of how students of Chinese feel when they travel from Shanghai to Taipei or from Guangzhou to Beijing.

The best thing is to learn the standard form which is understood universally. That way you should have little trouble making yourself understood, even if you can't always make out the responses you get.

The pronunciation used in this phrasebook is based on Mandarin as it is spoken in Beijing. As this is a prestigious form of the language, just as BBC English is in some parts of the English-speaking world, your ability to master its sounds will be applauded.

Pinyin 拼音

In 1958 the Chinese officially adopted a system of writing their language using the Roman alphabet. This is known as *pinyin*. There remain, however, a multitude of systems still in use.

In China you will see *pinyin* next to the Chinese characters on signs, shopfronts and advertising billboards. Don't expect Chinese people to be able to use pinyin, however. In the countryside and the smaller towns you may not see a single pinyin sign anywhere. This is where the script included in this book comes in handy.

Tones 声调

For speakers of English the sounds of Chinese are quite easy to reproduce. There are relatively few of them and many of them have equivalents in English. A little more difficult is the pronunciation of the words using the correct tone. In Chinese there are many words which are spelt and pronounced in exactly the same way, but mean something quite different. The way the words are distinguished is by the tone used when pronouncing it. English frequently employs tones but we use this tonal quality for emphasis or emotion

For example, it's no good just saying *tang* if you're ordering soup in a restaurant. Unless you pronounce the word in an unchanging high pitch, you could find yourself being given sugar, which is also *tang*, but pronounced in a rising tone.

There are four basic tones in Mandarin Chinese which are indicated by a diacritic above a letter – high (▬), rising (╱), falling-rising (﹀) and falling (╲). We can say that there is a fifth which is no tone at all. The word *ma* can have four different meanings depending on the tone:

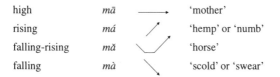

high	*mā*	⟶	'mother'
rising	*má*	╱	'hemp' or 'numb'
falling-rising	*mǎ*	﹀	'horse'
falling	*mà*	╲	'scold' or 'swear'

PRONUNCIATION

Vowels   韵母

a	as in 'f**a**ther'
ai	as in 'b**uy**'
ao	as in 'n**ow**'
e	as in 'f**ur**'
ei	as in 'd**ay**'
i	as in 's**ee**'; more like the 'e' in 'h**e**r' before **c, ch, r, s, sh, z** or **zh**
ian	as in 'y**en**'
ie	as in 'y**es**'
iu	as in 'y**eo**man'
o	as in '**o**r'
ou	as in 'l**ow**'
u	as in 'fl**u**te'; like **ü** when preceded by **q, j, x** or **y**
ü	as the French *'tu'* or the German *'für'*; place your lips as if you were going to whistle and say 'ee'
ui	as in 'w**ay**'
uo	as in 'w**ar**'

Consonants   声母

You'll notice that several of the consonants are pronounced the same way even though they are different letters. This is because of the way they combine with other sounds: **ci**, for example, sounds a little like 'tsuh', while **qi** sounds like 'tsee'. Similar pairs are **s** and **x**, and **zh** and **j**. All consonanst not listed here are pronounced as they would be in standard English.

c	as in 'ca**t**s'
h	a guttural sound like the 'ch' in 'lo**ch**' or the standard German *'ich'*

PRONUNCIATION

j	as in 'jeans'
q	as in 'cheque'
r	as in English but much softer; say 'r' but touch the roof of your mouth with the tip of your tongue so that it sounds something like the 's' in 'pleasure'
x	as in 'sock'
z	as in 'fads'
zh	as in 'jewel'

Grammar

语法

Chinese grammar, compared with English grammar is really quite simple. There are no verb conjugations, no plurals, no articles ('a/the') and, at an elementary level, has a sentence order similar to English.

Word Order
句子和词序

Like English, Chinese word order is subject-verb-object. For example, the sentence 'I study Chinese' follows exactly the same order in Chinese:

I study Chinese.   *wǒ xué hànyǔ*

As in English, adjectives precede the nouns they describe:

the big hotel   *dà fàndiàn*

Nouns
名词

Nouns are usually made up of two words (characters), called 'compounds', and have no masculine/feminine or plural forms:

restaurant   *fàn guǎn*
restaurants   *fàn guǎn*

13

Pronouns   代名词

I/me	*wǒ*
you	*nǐ*
she/her	*tā*
he/him	*tā*
it	*tā*
we/us	*wǒmen*
you (pl)	*nǐmen*
they/them	*tāmen*

Demonstrative Pronouns

this	*zhèige*	that	*nèige*
these	*zhèixiē*	those	*nèixiē*

Verbs   动词

When a Chinese speaker uses the verb 'to eat' *(chī)*, for example,
it doesn't change according to the subject or tense. There are no
'eats', 'eaten' or 'ate', just 'eat'. Past or future is normally
indicated by using an expression of time:

> Yesterday I ate fish.   *wǒ zuótiān chī yú*
> (lit: I yesterday eat fish)

Similarly Chinese verbs don't alter according to the subject:

I eat	*wǒ chī*	we eat	*wǒmen chī*
you eat	*nǐ chī*	you (pl) eat	*nǐmen chī*
he/she/it eats	*tā chī*	they eat	*tāmen chī*

To Be

Although Chinese has an equivalent to the English verb 'to be', *shì*, it is not used in quite the same way as in English. Chinese only uses the verb *shì* when a noun is involved like in a sentence such as 'I am a student'. With adjectives, *shì* is dropped altogether – a Chinese speaker would say 'I hungry', not 'I am hungry':

I am a student.	*wǒ shì xuéshēng* (lit: I am student)
I am hungry.	*wǒ èle* (lit: I hungry)

Tense

Tense is indicated by expressions of time like 'yesterday', 'tomorrow', 'a while ago', and so on. However, Chinese does use the particle *le* to indicate such things as whether an action is completed or not. In many cases this corresponds to the English past tense:

He is going to Shanghai.	*tā qù shànghǎi* (lit: he go Shanghai)
He has gone to Shanghai.	*tā qùle shànghǎi* (lit: he go *le* Shanghai)

For things that you have experienced or that have happened some time in the unspecified past, Chinese uses the particle *guo*:

I have been to Hong Kong.	*wǒ qùguo xiānggǎng* (lit: I go *guo* Hong Kong)

GRAMMAR

Commands   命令式

Commands in Chinese are basically formed by giving emphasis to the verb:

> Go away!   *zǒu!*

Commands in the negative are formed by using *búyào* ('not want') or *bié*:

> Don't be noisy!   *bié chǎo!*
> Don't go!   *búyào zǒu!*

Negatives   否定式

There are basically two particles that are used for forming the negative in Chinese. The one you're most likely to need is *bu*, which is placed before verbs or adjectives:

> I am not going to   *wǒ búqù shànghǎi*
> Shanghai.   (lit: I not go Shanghai)
> It's not good.   *bùhǎo*
>   (lit: not good)

The particle *méi* is used to indicate a negative in the past tense:

> I didn't go to Shanghai.   *wǒ méi qù shànghǎi*
>   (lit: I not go Shanghai)

Yes & No   正反式

There are no specific words in Chinese for 'Yes' and 'No'. Usually, when the Chinese are asked a question, they repeat the verb used in the question to answer in the affirmative:

Are you going to Shanghai?   *nǐ qù shànghǎi ma?*

    Yes.   *qù*
                                    (lit: go)

    No.   *bú qù*
                                    (lit: no go)

Often you will hear Chinese using the word *duì* as an equivalent to yes – it literally means 'correct':

Are you going to Shanghai tomorrow?   *nǐ míngtiān qù shànghǎi ma?*
                                    (lit: you tomorrow go Shanghai?)

    Yes.   *duì, míngtiān qù*
                                    (lit: correct, tomorrow go)

When a question is in the past tense you can use the word *yǒu* to answer in the affirmative:

Have you studied Chinese?   *nǐ xuéle zhōngwén ma?*

    Yes.   *Yǒu*
                                    (lit: I have)

    No.   *Meiyǒu*
                                    (lit: I have not)

Questions   发问式

Questions in Chinese are usually formed by adding the particle *ma* to the end of the sentence:

    He goes to Shanghai.   *tā qù shànghǎi*
    Is he going to Shanghai?   *tā qù shànghǎi ma?*

Other Chinese question words include the following:

GRAMMAR

who	*shéi*	Who are you?
		nǐ shì shéi?
which	*něige*	Which place?
		něige dìfang?
what	*shénme*	What is this?
		zhèige shì shénme?
where	*nǎr*	Where is he going?
		tā qù nǎr?
how	*zěnme*	How do I get there?
		zěnmezǒu?
when	*shénme shíhou*	When do you go?
		nǐ shénme shíhou qù?

To say 'or', as in 'tea or coffee?', use the word *háishi*. Use it in exactly the same way as you would in English by placing it between the two choices:

Are you going to Shanghai or Beijing?
nǐ qù shànghǎi háishi qù běijīng?
(lit: you go Shanghai or go Beijing?)

Measure Words　数量词

In Chinese, when you talk about quantities of any noun it's important to put a 'measure word' between the number and the noun. Even though there are many different measure words, depending on the kind of noun being counted, the good news is that there is an all-purpose measure word, *ge*, that can be used in all circumstances:

three cups	*sānge bēizi*
	(lit: three *ge* cups)

The more serious student of Chinese should set about learning some of the more common specific measure words. Here are a few examples:

- thin, flat objects *zhāng*
  four tickets *sìzhāng piào*
- animals *zhī*
  two dogs *liǎngzhī gǒu*
- businesses (restaurants, etc) *jiā*
  five restaurants *wǔjiā fànguǎnr*

It's worth remembering that measure words are also required between prepositions and nouns:

that person	*nèige rén*
	(lit: that *ge* person)
this place	*zhèige dìfang*
	(lit: this *ge* place)

Comparison 比较式

Comparisons are easy in Chinese. They are made in the following way, using the word *bǐ*:

Beijing is bigger than Shanghai. — *běijīng bǐ shànghǎi dà* (lit: Beijing *bi* Shanghai big)

This one is cheaper than that one. — *zhèige bǐ nèige piányì* (lit: this *bi* that cheap)

Possession 所属

To show ownership or possession, place the word *de* between the pronoun and the noun:

my backpack — *wǒde bèibāo* (lit: I *de* backpack)

their room — *tāmende fángjiān* (lit: they *de* room)

Quantity 数量

all	*dōu*
every	*měige*
enough	*gòule*
many/much	*duō*
little/few	*shǎo*
a bit	*yìdiǎnr*
several	*jǐge*

Some Useful Words 应用词汇

about	*chàbuduō*
and	*hé*

GRAMMAR

after	*yǐhòu*
at	*zài*
because	*yīnwei*
before	*yǐqián*
for	*wèi le*
from	*cóng*
if	*yàoshi/rúguǒ*
to	*dào*
towards	*wǎng*
with	*gēn*

GRAMMAR

Greetings & Civilities

交际

Greetings 问侯

The all-purpose greeting in China is:

Hello.
    nǐ hǎo 你好!
    nín hǎo (more polite) 您好!

Chinese has many other greetings but these are used more for people you are already acquainted with. Early in the morning, up to around 10 am, you might greet people with:

Good morning.
    zǎo 早!

But for the rest of the day there are no time-specific greetings, like 'Good afternoon' and 'Good evening' in English.

When the Chinese greet friends and acquaintances they're much more likely to use greetings such as:

How's it going?
    nǐ chīle ma? 你吃了吗?
    (lit: have you eaten?)

Where are you off to?
nǐ qù nǎr?   你去哪儿?

Another common way of greeting friends is to call out their names:

èi xiǎo zhāng!   唉! 小张
(lit: hey, young Zhang!)

Goodbyes   再见
Goodbye.	*zàijiàn*	再见!
Goodnight.	*wǎn'ān*	晚安!
See you tomorrow.	*míngtiān jiàn*	明天见

If you're seeing someone off on a long trip, the Chinese have an equivalent to 'bon voyage' that literally means 'smooth winds all the way':

Bon voyage!   *yílù shùn fēng!*   一路顺风

Civilities   寒喧

The Chinese don't say 'Please' and 'Thank you' quite as much as Westerners, but you won't offend anyone if you stick to the level of politeness which is customary in your own country. At the worst you'll just seem a bit of a stuffed shirt:

Thank you.	*xièxie*	谢谢
Not at all.	*bú xiè*	不谢
It was nothing.	*méi shénme*	没什么

If you don't want to appear too stuffy, it's worth remembering that a compliment goes much further than a formal 'Thank you' in China. If someone treats you to a meal, for example, you might say to them:

That was delicious.
hǎo chī jíle   好吃极了

If someone has done you a favour, a polite response is:

I've given you so much
trouble.
máfan nǐle   麻烦你了

Requests

When asking a question it is polite to start with the phrase *qǐng wèn* (lit: may I ask?). This expression is only used at the beginning of a sentence, never at the end:

Excuse me, where is the
railway station?
qǐng wèn, huǒchēzhàn
zài nǎr?   请问，火车站在哪儿？

If you want to squeeze past someone on a crowded bus the following is more appropriate:

Excuse me.
láo jià   劳驾

The same *qǐng* that is used in *qǐng wèn* means 'Please' when it is used on its own. It's used for making requests:

Please give me a hand.
  qǐng nǐ bāng wǒge máng　　　请你帮我个忙

Finally, *qǐng* may be used on its own, with the meaning of 'After you'.

Apologies

I'm sorry/Excuse me.
  duìbuqǐ　　　对不起
I'm so sorry.
  wǒ zhēn duìbuqǐ　　　我真对不起
It doesn't matter.
  méi guānxi　　　没关系

Forms of Address

称呼

After the revolution there was a move to make Chinese less hierarchical by replacing the old forms of address with the value-free term *tóngzhì* (comrade). This has, however, broken down to a large extent over recent years, and increasingly the Chinese are returning to old habits.

When the Chinese address each other they almost always use the surname and some kind of title. In the case of good friends or people whose relationship is fairly informal, this will probably take the form of a prefix such as *lǎo* (old) or *xiǎo* (young). Thus the young university student sitting opposite you on the train might be known to most of her friends as *xiǎo Zhāng*, while the middle-aged man in the corner might be *lǎo Liú*.

If, on the other hand, you are dealing with the Chinese on a less personal basis, it is useful to remember the importance of giving them 'face' by addressing them with a polite title. Unlike *xiǎo* and *lǎo* all other titles are placed after the person's surname.

Perhaps the most common and useful form of address is *shīfu*. Basically *shīfu* is a polite way of addressing someone who has a skill of some kind. Using it to address the person serving you in a restaurant or a department store, or the person selling tickets at the bus station, is a mild form of flattery that gives the addressee 'face' and helps to get things done.

The following are some of the more common forms of address used in China. Remember, they are placed *after* the person's name.

Dr	*dàifu*	大夫
driver	*sījī*	司机
manager	*jīnglǐ*	经理
master		师父
(lit: skilled person)	*shīfu*	
Miss	*xiǎojiě*	小姐
Mr	*xiānsheng*	先生
Mrs	*fūren*	夫人
Ms	*nǚshì*	女士
professor	*jiàoshòu*	教授
teacher	*lǎoshī*	老师

Names

It is the convention in China to place surnames *(xìng)*, before given names *(míng)*. In general, the surname consists of only one syllable, while the given name is made up of two.

Some of the more common surnames include: *lĭ, wáng, huáng, zhāng, liú* and *chén*. Given names are often one or two characters and are selected for their meaning, not for their sound. A particular name might be chosen because it embodies some quality the parents would like to see in their child. Names are even chosen for patriotic reasons. It's not uncommon in China to bump into people with names like *jiànguó* ('build up the country') and *wèijūn* ('defend the army').

Body Language   身体语言

Westerners needn't worry too much about upsetting anyone on this front while they are in China. The major differences between Western and Chinese body language apply equally to all Asian countries. The Chinese, for example, gesture with their palm downwards rather than upwards when they want someone to come to them. Public male-female body contact was once considered indecent but now is not uncommon to see young men or young women arm in arm.

GREETINGS & CIVILITIES

Small Talk

交谈

You'll have no shortage of opportunities to chat with the Chinese while you're in China. Most Chinese are reasonably curious about foreigners (to the extent that in the more out-of-the-way spots you'll attract small crowds of onlookers wherever you go). The only thing that holds the Chinese back in most cases is the lack of a common language. Remember the cultural differences and try not to get offended if someone asks you personal questions, such as how old you are and how much you earn.

Meeting People   会面
When exchanging names with the Chinese it is best to use the polite expression:

May I ask your name?
> *nín guì xìng?*   您贵姓?

This literally asks what is the 'honourable surname' of the person you are talking to. The other party will respond simply by giving his or her surname:

My (sur)name is Chen.
> *wǒ xìng chén*   我姓陈

You can follow this up with the question:

How should I address you?
wǒ zěnme chēnghu nǐ?

我怎么称呼你？

To which most Chinese will respond by giving you either a *xiǎo* or a *lǎo* prefix. (see Greetings & Civilities, page 25)

Nationalities　　　　　　　　　　　　　国籍

Where are you from?
nǐ shi cóng nǎr láide?

你是从哪儿来的？

I'm from ...	*wǒ shì ... láide*	我是…来的
Australia	*àodàliyà*	澳大利亚
Canada	*jiā nádà*	加拿大
China	*zhōngguó*	中国
Denmark	*dānmài*	丹麦
England	*yīngguó*	英国
Europe	*ōuzhōu*	欧洲
France	*fǎguó*	法国
Germany	*déguó*	德国
Holland	*hélán*	荷兰
Ireland	*àiěrlán*	爱尔兰
Italy	*yìdàlì*	意大利
Japan	*rìběn*	日本
Mongolia	*měnggǔ*	蒙古
New Zealand	*xīnxīlán*	新西兰
Norway	*nuówēi*	挪威
Scotland	*sūgélán*	苏格兰
Singapore	*xīnjiāpō*	新加坡
South Africa	*nánfēi*	南非

SMALL TALK

Sweden	*ruìdiǎn*	瑞典
Switzerland	*ruìshì*	瑞士
Taiwan	*táiwān*	台湾
the USA	*měiguó*	美国
Wales	*wēiěrshì*	威尔士

Age　　　　　　　　　　　　年龄

How old are you?
nǐ jǐ suì? (for young children)　　你几岁?
nǐ dūo dà? (for everyone else)　　你多大?

I am ... years old.	*wǒ ... suì*	我...岁
18	*shíbā*	十八
25	*èrshíwǔ*	二十五

(See Numbers & Amounts, page 124 for your particular age)

Occupations　　　　　　　　工作

What do you do?　*nǐ zuò shénme*　你做什么工作?
　　　　　　　　gōngzuò?

I'm ...	*wǒ shì ...*	我是...
an actor	*yǎnyuán*	演员
an artist	*huàjiā*	画家

SMALL TALK

a business-person	*shāngrén*	商人
a doctor	*yīshēng*	医生
an engineer	*gōngchéngshī*	工程师
a journalist	*jìzhě*	记者
a lawyer	*lǜshī*	律师
a manual worker	*gōngrén*	工人
a mechanic	*jìgōng*	技工
a nurse	*hùshi*	护士
an office worker	*zhíyuán*	职员
a student	*xuésheng*	学生
a teacher	*jiàoshī*	教师
a writer	*zuòjiā*	作家
a waiter	*fúwùyuán*	服务员

Religion   宗教

What is your religion?
nǐ shì xìn shénme zōngjiàode?   你是信什么宗教的?

I am ...	*wǒ shì xìn ... de*	我是信...的
Buddhist	*fójiào*	佛教
Catholic	*tiānzhǔjiào*	天主教
Christian	*jīdūjiào*	基督教
Hindu	*yìndùjiào*	印度教
Jewish	*yóutàijiào*	犹太教
Muslim	*yīsīlánjiào*	伊斯兰教
Protestant	*xīnjiào*	新教

I'm not religious.
wǒ bu xìnjiào   我不信教

Family   家庭

Are you married?
nǐ jiéhūnle ma?
你结婚了吗？

No, I'm not.
hái méi ne
还没呢

I'm single.
wǒ hái méi jiéhūn
我还没结婚

Yes, I am/I'm married.
wǒ jiéhūnle
我结婚了

Is your husband/wife also here?
nǐde zhàngfu/qīzi yě zài zhèr ma?
你的丈夫/妻子也在这儿吗？

Do you have any children?
nǐ yǒu háizile ma?
你有孩子了吗？

No.
hái méi ne
还没呢

Yes, one.
yǒu yíge
有一个

Yes, two.
yǒu liǎnge
有两个

Yes, three.
yǒu sānge
有三个

I have a daughter.
wǒ yǒu ge nǚér
我有个女儿

I have a son.
wǒ yǒu ge érzi
我有个儿子

How many brothers and sisters do you have?
nǐ yǒu jǐ ge xiōngdì jiěmèi?
你有几个兄弟姐妹？

I don't have any brothers
or sisters.
wǒ méi yǒu xiōngdì jiěmèi

I have ...
wǒ yǒu ... ge

Do you have a boy/girlfriend?
nǐ yǒu meiyǒu nán/nǚpéngyou?

我没有兄弟姐妹

你有...个

你有没有男（女）
朋友?

Family Members
Chinese terms for kin can get very complicated as there are separate titles according to whether (for brothers and sisters) they are older or younger than the person using the term, or whether (for uncles, aunts, etc) they are maternal or paternal relations. For this reason we only include the words for immediate family members here.

SMALL TALK

mother	*mǔqin*	母亲
father	*fùqin*	父亲
son	*érzi*	儿子
daughter	*nǔér*	女儿
elder brother	*gēge*	哥哥
younger brother	*dìdi*	弟弟
elder sister	*jiějie*	姐姐
younger sister	*mèimei*	妹妹
husband	*zhàngfu*	丈夫
wife	*qīzi*	妻子

* Sometimes you will come across the gender-neutral term *àiren* (lit: loved one) for 'husband' or 'wife'. Be careful using it, however. In other parts of the Chinese-speaking world the term means 'lover' and has a definite illicit connotation that does not go down well among the puritanical Chinese.

Feelings　　　　　　　　　　　　　　　　感受

I am ...	*wǒ ...*	我...
angry	*shēngqìle*	生气了
cold	*juéde lěng*	觉得冷
happy	*gāoxìngle*	高兴了
hot	*juéde rè*	觉得热
hungry	*èle*	饿了
in a hurry	*yǒu jíshì*	有急事
sleepy	*juéde kùn*	觉得困
thirsty	*kěle*	渴了
tired	*lèile*	累了

| I'm sorry. (apology) | *duìbuqǐ* | 对不起 |
| I'm grateful. | *wǒ hěn gǎnxiè* | 我很感谢 |

Opinions　　　　　　　　　　　意见表达

Don't expect the Chinese to be as forthright with their opinions
as Westerners are.

I like ...	*wǒ xǐhuan ...*	我喜欢…
I don't like ...	*wǒ bù xǐhuan ...*	我不喜欢…
Do you like ...?	*nǐ xǐhuan ... ma?*	你喜欢…吗?
Chinese	*zhōng*	中
Western	*xī*	西
food	*cān*	餐
music	*yīnyuè*	音乐
travelling	*lǚyóu*	旅游

Very interesting!	*hěn yǒu yìsi!*	很有意思
Really?	*zhēnde?*	真的?
Amazing!	*zhēn liǎobuqǐ!*	真了不起
So so.	*mǎmǎhūhū*	马马虎虎

Language Problems　　　　　语言问题

I don't speak Chinese.		
wǒ bu huì jiǎng zhōngwén		我不会讲中文
Do you speak English?		
nǐ huì jiǎng yīngyǔ ma?		你会讲英语吗?

Would you say that again
please?
    qǐng nǐ zài shuō yíbiàn?   请你再说一遍
Could you speak more
slowly please?
    qǐng nǐ shuō màn yídiǎnr?   请你说慢一点，好吗？
Please point to the phrase in
this book.
    qǐng nǐ zài zhèi běn shūli   请你在这本书里指出
    zhǐchū yào shuōde huà   要说的话
Let me see if I can find it in
this book.
    ràng wǒ cháchá zhèi běn shūba   让我查查这本书吧
I understand.
    wǒ dǒng   我懂
I don't understand.
    wǒ bù dǒng   我不懂
What does this/that mean?
    zhè/nà shi shénme yìsi?   这/那是什么意思？

Some Useful Phrases   应用词句

What is this/that called?
    zhè/nà jiào shénme míngzi?   这/那叫什么名字？
Can I take a photo?
    wǒ kěyǐ zhào ge xiàng ma?   我可以照个相吗？
Sure.
    kěyǐ   可以
Do you live here?
    nǐ zhù zài zhèige dìfang ma?   你住在这个地方吗？
Yes, I live here.
    shìde, wǒ zhù zài zhèr   是的，我住在这儿

SMALL TALK

No, I don't live here.
  búshì, wǒ bú zhù zài zhèr
不是，我不住在这儿

It's beautiful, isn't it?
  hěnpiàoliàng shìma
很漂亮，是吗

That's interesting
  nàhěnyǒuqù
那很有趣

We love it here.
  wǒménhěnxǐhuānzhàr
我们很喜欢这儿

Really?
  zhēndema?
真的吗？

Never mind.
  méiguānxi
没关糸

No problem.
  méiwànt í
没问题

Sure.
  yídìng
一定

Maybe.
  kěnéng
可能

Lovely day, isn't it?
  tiāngìzhēnhǎo shìma
天气真好，是吗

What a cute baby!
  duōmekěāideháizia!
多么可爱的孩子啊

Getting Around

旅遊

There are three main tourist offices operating in China that can help you with travel bookings. The CITS (China International Travel Service) may sell hard-to-get tickets but, according to many travellers, the service is poor and prices are high. The CTS (China Travel Service) sells tickets and can also help with visas. The CYTS (China Youth Travel Service) offers the same services as the others and, as it must compete with these larger organisations, the service is often better but the prices are not necessarily cheaper.

What time does ... leave/arrive?	... jǐdiǎn kāi/dào?	...几点开/到?
the bus	qìchē	汽车
the train	huǒchē	火车
the plane	fēijī	飞机
the boat	chuán	船

I'd like to go to ...		
wǒ xiǎng qù ...		我想去...
How much is it to go to ...?		
qù ... duōshǎo qián?		去...多少钱?
How can I get to ...?		
zěnme qù ...?		怎么去...?

Is there another way to get
there?
yǒu biéde bànfa qù ma?　　　　　　　有别的办法去吗?

Finding Your Way 　　　　　　　　问路

Where is ...?　　　　　*... zài nǎr?*　　　　...在哪儿?
  the bus station　　*qìchē zǒngzhàn*　　汽车总站
    (central)
  the bus stop　　　　*qìchē zhàn*　　　　汽车站
  the train station　　*huǒchē zhàn*　　　火车站
  the airport　　　　　*jīchǎng*　　　　　机场
  the subway station　*dìtie znàn*　　　　地铁站
  the ticket office　　*shòupiào chù*　　售票处

Excuse me, what direction
is ...?
qǐngwèn, ... něige fāngxiàng?　　请问...哪个方向?
Excuse me, am I going in the
right direction for ...?
qǐngwèn, qù ... zǒu zhèige　　　请问去...走这个方向
fāngxiàng duìma?　　　　　　　对吗?
Is it far?
yuǎnbuyuǎn?　　　　　　　　　远不远?
Yes, it's far.
hěn yuǎn　　　　　　　　　　　很远
No, it's not far.
bùyuǎn　　　　　　　　　　　　不远
Is it near here?
lí zhèr jìn ma?　　　　　　　　离这儿近吗?
Can I walk there?
wǒ kěyǐ zǒulù ma?　　　　　　我可以走路吗?

Is it difficult to find?
   hǎobuhǎo zhǎo?   好不好找？

What ... is this?	*zhè shi ...?*	这是...？
street	*nĕitiáo jiē*	哪条街
suburb	*nĕige jiāoqū*	哪个郊区

Directions   方向
When the Chinese give directions they almost invariably use the compass points.

north	*bĕi*	北
south	*nán*	南
east	*dōng*	东

west	*xī*	西
straight ahead	*yìzhí*	一直
upstairs	*lóushàng*	楼上
downstairs	*lóuxià*	楼下
right	*yòubiānr*	右边儿
left	*zuǒbiānr*	左边儿

Air 航空

The Civil Aviation Administration of China (CAAC) is the umbrella organisation of numerous airlines operating within China. Flights are now available to all corners of China. Foreigners have to pay a special foreigner's fare for CAAC tickets which is up to 2.5 times the Chinese price. Children over 12 years of age are required to pay a full adult's fare.

Is there a flight to ...?
  yǒu qù ... de fēijī ma? 有去...的飞机吗?

When is the next flight to ...?
  qù ... de xiàbān fēijī shì shénme shíhou qǐfēide? 去...的下班飞机是什么时候起飞的?

How long does the flight take?
  yào zuò dūocháng shíjiānde fēijī? 要坐多长时间的飞机?

I would like to book a ticket to ...
  wǒ xiǎng dìng yìzhāng qù ... de piào 我想订一张去...的票

I would like a one-way ticket.
  wǒ xiǎngyào yìzhāng dānchéng piào 我想要一张单程票

I would like a return ticket.

	wǒ xiǎngyào yìzhāng láihuí piào	我想要一张来回票

Please show your...	*qǐng náchu nǐde ...*	请拿出你的...
boarding pass	*dēngjī kǎ*	登机卡
customs declaration	*hǎiguān shēnbàodān*	海关申报单
passport	*hùzhào*	护照

cancel	*qǔxiāo*	取消
confirm	*quèrèn*	确认
economy ticket	*pǔtōng piào*	普通票
1st-class ticket	*tóuděng piào*	头等票
smoking	*xīyānqū*	吸烟区
nonsmoking	*fēixīyānqū*	非吸烟区

Bus   公共汽车

The best thing about long-distance bus travel in China is that during the meal breaks you get to stop and poke around in little towns and villages that you wouldn't normally get the chance to see. On the negative side, the buses are generally uncomfortable and crowded and breakdowns are frequent. Government-run buses seem to be safer than privately run ones.

In the cities, maps of bus routes are available from hotels, local bookstores and travel offices, although everything is usually in Chinese characters. These maps are called *shìqū dìtú* (市区地图) or *jiāotōng dìtú* (交通地区).

Before boarding a bus it might be a good idea to have someone write down the name of the place you want to go to in Chinese characters. You can show this to the driver or conductor.

Does this bus go to ...?
zhèiliàng qìchē qù ... ma?

这辆汽车...吗?

Which bus goes to ...?
něiliàng qìchē qù ...?

哪辆汽车去...?

How frequently do the
buses run?
dūocháng shíjiān yìbān?

这辆汽车多长时间一
班?

Can you tell me when we
get to ...?
*wǒmen dào ... de shíhou, nǐ
néngbunéng jiào wǒ yíxià?*

我们到...的时候能不
能叫我一下?

I want to get off!
xià chē!

下车!

When is the ... bus? *... bān chē shénme
shíhou lái?*

...班车什么时候来?

next	*xià*	下
first	*tóu*	头
last	*mò*	末

Train

铁路

Trains are reliable, fast and, with the exception of the hard-seat class, reasonably comfortable. There are train services around every province in the country except Tibet. Buying tickets from railway stations, although cheap, often involves long queues and frustration. Hard-seat tickets are usually easy to get at short notice but for sleepers, it may be best to book at tourist offices. Black market tickets are rife but make sure you are buying a genuine ticket and be aware that authorities in major cities will fine you for using them.

There are four classes of railway tickets available:

hard-seat	*yìngzuò*	硬座
hard-sleeper	*yìngwò*	硬卧
soft-seat	*ruǎnzuò*	软座
soft-sleeper	*ruǎnwò*	软卧

Chinese trains also come in local, slow, fast and express forms:

local train	*pǔtōng chē*	普通车
slow train	*màn chē*	慢车
fast train	*kuài chē*	快车
express train	*tèkuài chē*	特快车

Buying Tickets

Where is the ticket office?
  shòupiàochù zài nǎr? 售票处在哪儿?

I would like a (hard-seat)
ticket to ...
  wǒ xiǎng mǎi yìzhāng qù ... de 我想买一张去…的
  (yìngzuò) piào （硬座）票

How much is a (hard-seat)
fare to ...?
  qù ... de (yìngzuò) piào 去…的（硬座）票
  dūoshǎo qián? 多少钱?

Is it an express train?
  shì tèkuài huǒchē ma? 是特快火车吗?

I'd like ... *wǒyàoyíge ...* 我要一个…
  an upper berth *shàngpù* 上铺
  a middle berth *zhōngpù* 中铺
  a bottom berth *xiàpù* 下铺

I would like to upgrade my
ticket.
  wǒ xiǎng bǔpiào 我想补票

I want to change to *wǒ xiǎng huàn ...* 我想换…
a ...
  hard-sleeper *yìngwò* 硬卧
  soft-seat *ruǎnzuò* 软座
  soft-sleeper *ruǎnwò* 软卧

Some Useful Words & Phrases

adult's ticket *dàrén piào* 大人票
child's ticket *értóng piào* 儿童票

dining car	*cānchē*	餐车
no smoking	*jìnyān*	禁烟
one-way (ticket)	*dānchéng (piào)*	单程（票）
railway station	*huǒchē zhàn*	火车站
return (ticket)	*láihuí (piào)*	来回（票）
subway	*dìtiě*	地铁
subway station	*dìtiě zhàn*	地铁站
train	*huǒchē*	火车
train timetable	*lièchē shíkèbiǎo*	列车时刻表

Where are we now?
wǒmen xiànzài zài nǎr?　　　　　我们现在在哪儿?

Can you tell me when we get
to ...?
dào ... de shíhou qǐng nín jiào　　到...的时候请您叫我
wǒ yíxià hǎo ma?　　　　　　　　一下好吗?

Excuse me, this is my seat.
duìbuqǐ, zhè shi wǒde wèizi　　　　对不起! 这是我的位子

Taxi 出租汽车

Long-distance taxis are usually booked through travel offices or hotels. The fees asked are excessive and you will have to negotiate. It is not difficult to find private taxi drivers who will charge much less.

All over China you'll find the poor person's taxi; the rickshaw, in both its leg-powered and fossil fuel-powered varieties. These are far cheaper than taxis, but unlike taxis they don't have meters. All prices must be bargained. Unfortunately, the Chinese, unlike their neighbours in many other Asian countries, are not always friendly bargainers, and things can get nasty if you push too hard – stay relaxed and move on if you start getting bad vibes.

I'd like to get a taxi.
wǒ xiǎng jiào chūzūqìchē
我想叫出租汽车

Driver, could you take me to ...?
sījǐ, nǐ néng bǎ wǒ sòngdao ... ma?
司机你能把我送到 ...吗？

To ..., please!
qǐng kāidào ...!
请开到...

Can you wait for me?
nǐ néng děng wǒ ma?
你能等我吗？

I'll be right back.
wǒ mǎshàng jiù huílai
我马上就回来

I'll be back in ...
wǒ ... jiù huílai
我...就回来

How much do I owe you?
nà yào dūoshao qián?
那要多少钱？

Instructions

Turn to the left.
wàng zuǒ guǎi
往左拐

Turn to the right.
wàng yòu guǎi
往右拐

Go straight ahead.
yìzhí zǒu
一直走

This is the wrong way.
zǒu cuò lùle
走错路了

Here is fine, thank you.
zài zhèr tíng jiùhǎole
在这儿停就好了

Stop at the next corner, please.
qǐng tíng zài xiàge lùkǒu
请停在下个路口

Stop at the next street on the
left/right, please.
    qǐng tíng zài zuǒ/yòu biānde 请停在左/右边的下个
    xiàge lùkǒu 路口
Please slow down.
    qǐng màn yìdiǎnr 请慢一点儿
Please hurry.
    qǐng kuài yìdiǎnr 请快一点儿
Please wait here.
    qǐng liú zài zhèr 请留在这儿

Bargaining

Remember the important concept of 'face' when you're bargaining for anything in China. Any direct challenge (such as 'don't try to cheat me', or words to that effect) is going to result in a situation where somebody has to lose face. This is sure to raise the odds and increase the excitement, but it could also lead to some unpleasantness. Keep smiling and try to keep your cool.

How much (is it) to ...?	去...多少钱?
qù ... dūoshao qián?	
That's too expensive!	太贵了
tài guìle!	
How about ...? (use fingers to indicate amount)	
... hǎobuhǎo?	...好不好?
That's not right, is it?	我看不对吧
wǒ kàn búduìba?	
OK.	好
hǎo	

Boat　　　　　　　　　　　　　　客船

With increased and improved bus and plane transport, the boats in China are disappearing fast. There are times, however, when boats are the easiest way of getting around. Famous river journeys include the Yangtse River trip from Chongqing to Wuhan, and the Li River from Canton to Wuzhou, a popular means of getting to Guilin.

I'd like a ... ticket to (Wuhan).	*wǒ xiǎng mǎi yìzhāng qù (wǔhàn) de ... piào*	我想买一张去（武汉）的...票
2nd class	*èrděng*	
3rd class	*sānděng*	二等
4th class	*sìděng*	三等
		四等

How long will we stop here?	我们在这儿停多久?
wǒmen zài zhèr tíng dūojiǔ?	
What time should we be back on board?	我们应该几点回来?
wǒmen yīnggāi jǐdiǎn huílái?	

Could you write it down for
me please?
nǐ néngbunéng xiěxiàlái?   你能不能写下来？
I'm feeling a bit seasick.
wǒ yǒudiǎnr yūnchuán   我有点儿晕船

Bicycle   自行车

The best means of local transport is the bicycle. More and more
places are providing facilities for foreigners to rent bicycles,
though many require a passport as proof of your intention to bring
the bike back.

Where can I hire a bicycle?
wǒ zài nǎr néng zū zìxíngchē?   我在哪儿能租自行车？
I'd like to hire a bicycle.
wǒ xiǎng zū yíliàng zìxíngchē   我想租一辆自行车
How much is the rental?
zūjīn yào duōshao?   租金要多少？
I'll return it tomorrow.
wǒ míngtiān huán gěi nǐ   我明天还给你
How much is it per day?
yìtiān duōshao qián?   一天多少钱？
How much is the deposit?
yājīn yào duōshao?   押金要多少？
Where is the bicycle parking
lot?
zìxíngchē cúnfàngchù zài nǎr?   自行车存放处在哪儿？

Some Useful Phrases   应用词句

Excuse me.
láojià   劳驾

Can I reserve a place?
wǒ néngbunéng dìng wèizi?

我能不能订位子?

Are there any seats left?
háiyǒu wèizi ma?

还有位子吗?

How long does it take?
yào dūojiǔ?

要多久?

How much is it?
yào dūoshao qián?

要多少钱?

Is it a direct route?
yìzhí zǒu ma?

一直走吗?

Is this seat taken?
yǒu rén zuò zhèige wèizi ma?

有人坐这个位子吗?

I want to get off at ...
wǒ yào zài ... xià chē

我要在...下车

Where is the toilet?
cèsuǒ zài nǎr?

厕所在哪儿?

Some Useful Words

应用词汇

above	*shàngbiān*	上边
address	*dìzhǐ*	地址
around here	*zhèli fùjìn*	这里附近
arrive	*dào*	到
below	*xiàbiān*	下边
bicycle	*zìxíngchē*	自行车
boat	*chuán*	船
bus stop	*qìchē zhàn*	汽车站
cabin	*kècāng*	客舱
Careful!	*xiǎoxīn diǎnr!*	小心点儿
early	*zǎo*	早
far	*yuǎn*	远
fastest route	*zuì kuàide lù*	最快的路

ferry	*dùchuán*	渡船
1st class	*tóuděng*	头等
map	*dìtú*	地图
motorbike	*mótuōchē*	摩托车
near	*jìn*	近
over there	*zài nèibiān*	在那边
pedicab	*sānlúnchē*	三轮车
port	*mǎtóu*	码头
seat	*zuòwèi*	座位
2nd class	*èrděng*	二等
Stop!	*tíng!*	停!
subway (in Beijing)	*dìtiě*	地铁
ticket	*piào*	票
timetable	*shíkèbiǎo*	时刻表
Wait!	*děng yìhuǐr!*	等一会儿

Accommodation

住宿

If you're staying in luxury hotels, it is unlikely that you will need to use Mandarin very often. If, on the other hand, you're travelling around China cheaply, you'll need to know some phrases to negotiate cheaper rooms or a place in a dormitory.

You will find three main types of accommodation in China – expensive hotels aimed at tourists and businesspeople, rambling mid-priced places that cater to overseas Chinese and high-ranking officials, and very basic, often Chinese-only, places with rock-bottom prices. Budget travellers usually find rooms or dormitories in hotels belonging to the last two categories.

- Top-range hotels and guesthouses in China come in the following two categories and cater for foreigners, overseas and Chinese and affluent locals:

  bīnguǎn   宾馆
  fàndiàn   饭店

- Hotels, sometimes available to foreigners, and are often expensive:

  lǚguǎn   旅馆

- Very much bottom of the range and inaccessible for foreigners in most circumstances are:

zhāodàisuǒ	招待所
lǔshè	旅社

Finding Accommodation 寻找旅馆

Where is ...?	... *zài nǎr?*	...在哪儿?
a hotel	*lǔ guǎn*	旅馆
a guesthouse	*zhāodàisuǒ lǔshè*	招待所/旅社

I am looking for ...	*wǒ zhǎo yìjiā ...*	我找一家...
a cheap hotel	*piányìde lǔguǎn*	便宜的旅馆
a good hotel	*hǎo lǔguǎn*	好旅馆
a nearby hotel	*lí zhèr bùyuánde lǔguǎn*	离这儿不远的旅馆

Could you write down the address for me please?
nǐ néngbunéng bǎ dìzhǐ xiěxiàlai gěi wǒ?

你能不能把地址写下来给我?

Is it possible to walk from here?
cóng zhèr zǒulù kěyǐqùma?

从这儿走路可以去吗?

Yes, it's not far.
kěyǐ, bùyuǎn

可以,不远

No, it's a long way.
bùkěyǐ, hěn yuǎn

不可以,很远

At the Hotel
Checking In

旅馆服务

Do you have any rooms available?
    nǐmen yǒumeiyǒu kōngfáng?
你们有没有空房？

I'd like ...	*wǒ xiǎng yào...*	我想要…
a single room	*yìjiān dānrénfáng*	一间单人房
a double room	*yìjiān shuāngrénfáng*	一间双人房
a room with a bathroom	*yǒu yùshìde fángjiān*	有浴室的房间
to share a dorm	*zhù sùshè*	住宿舍
a bed	*yí ge chuángwèi*	一个床位

I want a room with a ...	*wǒ yào yíjiàn yǒu ... de fángjiān*	我要一间有…的房间
bathroom	*yùshì*	浴室
shower	*línyù*	淋浴
telephone	*diànhuà*	电话
television	*diànshì*	电视
window	*chuānghu*	窗户

Is there ...?	*yǒumeiyǒu ...?*	有没有...?
air-conditioning	*kōngtiáo shèbei*	空调设备
heating	*nuǎnqì*	暖气

How much does it cost?
yào dūoshǎo qián? — 要多少钱？

Do you give a discount for
students?
duì liúxuéshēng yǒumeiyǒu — 对留学生有没有优惠？
yōuhuì?

Can I see the room?
wǒ néng kànkan fángjiān ma? — 我能看看房间吗？

Are there any others?
háiyǒu biéde fángjiān ma? — 还有别的房间吗？

Are there any cheaper ones?
yǒuméiyǒu piányì yìdiǎnde? — 有没有便宜一点儿的？

It's fine, I'll take it.
hǎo, wǒ jiù yào zhèijiān — 好，我就要这一间

I'm going to stay for	*wǒ dǎsuàn zhù ...*	我打算住...
one night	*yíge wǎnshang*	一个晚上
two nights	*liǎngge wǎnshang*	二个晚上
three nights	*sānge wǎnshang*	三个晚上
one week	*yíge xīngqī*	一个星期

I'm a student.
wǒ shi xuésheng — 我是学生

Here's my student card.
zhè shi wǒde xuéshēngzhèng — 这是我的学生证

I'm not sure how long I'm staying.
wǒ hái bùzhīdào yào zhù dūocháng shíjiān

我还不知道要住多长时间

Is there a lift?
yǒumeiyǒu diàntī?

有没有电梯？

Where's the bathroom?
yùshì zài nǎr?

浴室在哪儿？

Is there hot water all day?
yìtiān dōu yǒu rèshuǐ ma?

一天都有热水吗？

When is the heating turned on?
shénme shíhou cái yǒu nuǎnqì?

什么时候才有暖气？

Should I leave my key at reception when I go out?
wǒ chūqùde shíhou, shìbushi yào bǎ yàoshi liúxia?

我出去的时候是不是要把钥匙留下？

Complaints

I don't like this room.
wǒ bù xǐhuan zhèijiān fángjiān

我不喜欢这间房间

It's too ...	*tài ...*	太...
expensive	*guìle*	贵了
hot	*rèle*	热了
cold	*lěngle*	冷了
big	*dàle*	大了
small	*xiǎole*	小了
dark	*ànle*	暗了
noisy	*chǎole*	吵了

Do you have ... room?	*yǒumeiyǒu ... de fángjiān?*	有没有...的房间
another	*qítā*	其它
a cheaper	*gèng piányì*	更便宜
a better	*gèng hǎo*	更好

The ... doesn't work.	*... huài le*	...坏了
air-conditioner	*kōngtiáo shèbei*	空调设备
light	*dēng*	灯
shower	*línyù*	淋浴
tap (faucet)	*shuǐ lóngtóu*	水龙头
toilet	*cèsuǒ*	厕所

Can you get it repaired?
  néng xiū ma? 能修吗?
My room number is ...
  wǒ ... hào fáng jiān 我...号房间
I'd like to change to another room.
  wǒ xiǎng huàn yíge fángjiān 我想换一个房间

Requests

Do you have a safe where I
can store my valuables?

*nǐmen yǒumeiyǒu cún guìzhòng
dōngxide bǎoxiǎnxiāng?*

你们有没有存贵重东
西的保险箱?

Can you store this/these for
me?

*nǐmen néngbunéng bāng wǒ bǎ
zhèi ge/xiē dōngxi cún zài
bǎoxiǎnxiāngli?*

你们能不能帮我把这
个/些东西存在保险
箱里?

Is there somewhere to wash
clothes?

yǒumeiyǒu xǐ yīfude dìfang?

有没有洗衣服的地方?

Is there a telephone I can use?

*zhèr yǒumeiyǒu
gōngyòngdiànhuà?*

这儿有没有公用电话?

Is there a dining room?

zhèr yǒumeiyǒu shítáng?

这儿有没有食堂?

Please wake me up at (6.30
am) tomorrow.

*qǐng míngtiān zǎoshang
(liùdiǎnbàn) jiàoxǐng wǒ*

请明天早上（六点半）
叫醒我

The room needs to be
cleaned.

*néngbunéng dǎsǎo yíxià wǒde
fángjiān*

能不能打扫一下我的
房间?

Please change the sheets.

qǐng huàn chuángdān

请换床单

Please make up my bill.

qǐng bāng wǒ jiézhàng

请帮我结帐

ACCOMMODATION

I need ...	wǒ xiǎngyào ...	我想要…
some hangers	jǐge guàyījià	几个挂衣架
some soap	yíkuài féizào	一块肥皂
a towel	yìtiáo máojīn	一条毛巾

Checking Out 退房

We would like to check out ...	wǒmen ... yào zǒu	我们…要走
now	xiànzài	现在
at noon today	jīntiān zhōngwǔ	今天中午
tomorrow	míngtiān	明天

I'm returning ...	wǒ ... huílai	我…回来
tomorrow	míngtiān	明天
the day after tomorrow	hòutiān	后天
in a few days	jǐtiān yǐhòu	几天以后

Can I leave my bags here?
nǐmen néngbunéng bāng wǒ bǎoguǎn yíxià xíngli?

你们能不能帮我保管一下行李？

Some Useful Words 应用词汇

address	dìzhǐ	地址
air-conditioning	kōngtiáo shèbèi	空调设备
babysitter	línshí bǎomǔ	临时保姆
bathroom	yùshì	浴室

ACCOMMODATION

bed	*chuáng*	床
bill	*zhàngdān*	帐单
blanket	*tǎnzi*	毯子
bucket	*shuǐtǒng*	水桶
candle	*làzhú*	腊烛
chair	*yǐzi*	椅子
clean	*gānjìng*	干净
cot	*értóngchuáng*	儿童床
dining room	*cānfīng*	餐厅
dirty	*zāng*	脏
double bed	*shuāngrénchuáng*	双人床
electricity	*diàn*	电
fan (electric)	*diànshàn*	电扇
key	*yàoshi*	钥匙
lift (elevator)	*diàntī*	电梯
light bulb	*dēngpào*	灯泡
lock (n)	*suǒ*	锁
mattress	*chuángdiàn*	床垫
mirror	*jìngzi*	镜子
pillow	*zhěntou*	枕头
quiet	*jìng*	静
reception	*fúwùtái*	服务台
sheet	*chuángdān*	床单
shower	*línyù*	淋浴
soap	*féizào*	肥皂
suitcase	*yīxiāng*	衣箱
table	*zhūozi*	桌子
toilet	*cèsuǒ*	厕所
toilet paper	*wèishēngzhǐ*	卫生纸
towel	*máojīn*	毛巾
window	*chuānghu*	窗户

Laundry   洗衣服务

Many Chinese hotels have a laundry service, and most of the larger, more expensive ones have a drycleaning service as well.

ACCOMMODATION

Could I have these clothes ..., please?	*qǐng bǎ zhèixiē yīfu ...*	请把这些衣服...
washed	*xǐ gānjìng*	洗干净
ironed	*yùn hǎo*	熨好
dry-cleaned	*gānxǐ*	干洗

When will they be ready?
shénme shíhou néng xǐhǎo?   什么时候能洗好?

I need it ...	*wǒ ... xūyào*	我...需要
today	*jīntiān*	今天
tomorrow	*míngtiān*	明天
the day after tomorrow	*hòutiān*	后天

Is my laundry ready?
wǒde yīfu xǐhǎole ma?   我的衣服洗好了吗?
This isn't mine.
zhè búshì wǒde   这不是我的
There's a piece missing.
shǎole yíjiàn   少了一件

Around Town

市内

Most modern Chinese cities bear little resemblance to the China of the Western imagination – mazes of winding alleyways lined with picturesque wooden dwellings. Modern China is a world of boulevards and concrete, and most of the old buildings still standing are those built by Westerners in cities like Shanghai, Wuhan and Tianjin. Perhaps the one advantage of the virtual reconstruction of China, that has taken place over the last 40 years, is that the grid-like street plan of many Chinese cities makes finding your way around a little simpler, even if there often isn't a lot to look at while you're doing so.

In many cities nowadays it is best to get around by bicycle. This means you won't have to resort to the horribly overcrowded public transport system, where theft by stealth is becoming an everfrequent occurrence.

I want to go to the ...	*wǒ xiǎng qù ...*	我想去…
Excuse me, where is the nearest ...?	*qǐng wèn, zuìjìnde ... zài nǎr?*	请问,最近的…在哪儿?
bank	*yínháng*	银行
bus stop	*qìchēzhàn*	汽车站

(Australian) embassy	*(àodàlìyà) de dàshǐguǎn*	（澳大利亚）的 大使馆
post office	*yóujú*	邮局
train station	*huǒchēzhàn*	火车站
underground station	*dìtiě zhàn*	地铁站

I am looking for ...	*wǒ zhǎo...*	我找…
the art gallery	*měishùguǎn*	美术馆
the bank	*yínháng*	银行
the church	*jiàotáng*	教堂
the city centre	*shì zhōngxīn*	市中心
my hotel	*wǒde lǚguǎn*	我的旅馆
the market	*shìchǎng*	市场
the museum	*bówùguǎn*	博物馆
CITS	*zhōngguó guójìlǚxíngshè*	中国国际旅行社
the university	*dàxué*	大学
the zoo	*dòngwuyuán*	动物园

When does it open?
jǐdiǎn kāi mén?   几点开门？

When does it close?
jǐdiǎn guan mén?   几点关门？

At the Post Office　　　　　　邮局

The postal service in China is reasonably efficient, but it's a good idea to save any parcels for the big cities, where they have a bit more experience in dealing with such things. Don't expect any English to be spoken in post offices. Theoretically, postal rates are uniform throughout China, but you will find that they differ from post office to post office.

I would like to send ...	*wǒ xiǎng jì ...*	我想寄...
a letter	*yìfēng xìn*	一封信
a postcard	*yìzhāng míngxìnpiàn*	一张明信片
a parcel	*yíjiàn bāoguǒ*	一件包裹

I would like to send a telegram.
wǒ xiǎng fāge diànbào　　　　我想发个电报

I would like to send this letter to ...
wo xiǎng bǎ zhèifēng xìn jì dào ...　　　　我想把这封信寄到...

How much is it to send it to ...?	*jìdào ... yào dūoshao qián?*	寄到...要多少钱?
Australia	*àodàlìyà*	澳大利亚
England	*yīngguó*	英国
the USA	*měiguó*	美国

aerogram	*hángkōngxìnjiàn*	航空信件
airmail	*hángkōng*	航空

registered mail	*guàhàoxìn*	挂号信
envelope	*xìnfēng*	信封
parcel	*bāoguǒ*	包裹
poste restante	*yóujiàn dàilíngchù*	邮件待领处
stamp	*yóupiào*	邮票
surface mail	*píngyóu*	平邮

Telephone

Most hotel rooms have phones from which local calls are free. You can place domestic and international long-distance calls from telecommunications offices. Reverse-charges calls are often cheaper than calls paid for in China.

I would like to make a long-distance call to ...

   wǒ xiǎng gěi ... dǎge chángtú diànhuà — 我想给...打个长途电话

The number is ...

   diànhuà hàomǎ shi ... — 电话号码是...

How much is it per minute?

   yìfēnzhōng yào dūoshao qián? — 一分钟要多少钱？

Hello, do you speak English?

   wéi, nǐ huì jiǎng yīngwén ma? — 喂，你会讲英文吗？

Hello, is (Mr Li) there?

   wéi, (lǐ xiānshēng) zài ma? — 喂，（李先生）在吗？

He/She's not here.

   tā búzài — 他不在

Yes, hang on a minute.

   tā zài, qǐng děng yìhuǎr — 他在，请等一会儿

Operator, I've been cut off.

   zǒngjī, xiàn duànle — 总机，线断了

AROUND TOWN

telephone	*diànhuà*	电话
public telephone	*gōngyòng diànhuà*	公用电话
person-to-person call	*jiàorén diànhuà*	叫人电话
reverse charges (collect) call	*duìfāng fùkuǎn diànhuà*	对方付款电话
engaged	*zhàn xiàn*	占线
operator	*zǒngjī*	总机

At the Bank 银行

AROUND TOWN

The Chinese currencyis known as Renminbi (RMB) or 'People's Money'. Formally the basic unit of RMB is the *yuan*, which is divided into ten *jiao*. Colloquially the yuan is referred to as *kuai* and jiao as *mao*.

As well as at banks and foreign exchange counters in large hotels, you can change money at many Friendship Stores and some of the big department stores. US dollars are still the easiest to change. Travellers' cheques are useful as the exchange rate is often better than what you get for cash.

I would like to change some money.
    wǒ xiǎng duìhuàn diǎnr qián   我想兑换点儿钱
I would like to change travellers' cheques.
    wǒ xiǎng duìhuàn lǚxíng zhīpiào   我想兑换旅行支票
What is the exchange rate?
    duìhuǎnlǜshì duō shǎo?   兑换率是多少?

Can you cash a personal cheque?
kěyǐ duìhuàn sīrén zhīpiào ma? 可以兑换私人支票吗?

I'm expecting some money from ...
wǒ zhèngzài děng cóng ... 我正在等从...回来的
huílaide yìbǐ qián 一笔钱

Could you write it down for me?
nǐ néngbunéng xiěxiàlai gěi wǒ? 你能不能写下来给我

I would like to change some ...	*wǒ xiǎng duìhuàn diǎnr ...*	我想兑换点...
US$	*měiyuán*	美元
UK£	*yīngbàng*	英镑
Hong Kong $	*gǎngbì*	港币
Canadian $	*jiābì*	加币
Australian $	*àobì*	澳币
Deutschmarks	*mǎkè*	马克
Japanese yen	*rìyuán*	日元

bankdraft	*yínhánghuìpiào*	银行汇票
banknote	*chāopiào*	钞票
cash	*xiànjīn*	现金
cashier	*chūnàyuán*	出纳员
credit card	*xìnyòngkǎ*	信用卡
exchange	*duìhuàn*	兑换
loose change	*língqián*	零钱
signature	*qiānmíng*	签名

Sightseeing 观光

Excuse me, what's ...?	qǐngwèn, nèige ... shi shénme?	请问，那个...是什么？
that building	jiànzhùwù	建筑物
that monument	jìniànwù	纪念物
that park	gōngyuán	公园

Do you have a local map?
yǒu dāngdì dìtú ma?
有当地地图吗？

Can I take photographs?
wǒ néngbunéng zhàoxiàng?
我能不能照相？

Can I take your photograph?
wǒ kěyǐ gěi nǐ zhàoxiàng ma?
我可以给你照相吗？

I'll send you the photos later.
yǐhòu wǒ bǎ zhàopiàn jì gěi nǐ
以后我把照片寄给你

Please write down your name and address.
qǐng bǎ nǐde míngzi hé dìzhǐ xièxiàlai
请把你的名字和地址写下来

What time does it open?
jǐdiǎn kāi mén?
几点开门？

What time does it close?
jǐdiǎn gūan mén?
几点关门？

art gallery	měishùguǎn	美术馆
ancient	gǔlǎode	古老的
beach	hǎitān	海滩
Buddhist temple	sì/miào	寺/庙
building	jiànzhùwù	建筑物
church	jiàotáng	教堂
free market	zìyóu shìchǎng	自由市场

market	*shìchǎng*	市场
monument	*jìniànbēi*	纪念碑
museum	*bówùguǎn*	博物馆
palace	*gōngdiàn*	宫殿
Taoist temple	*guàn*	观
university	*dàxué*	大学

AROUND TOWN

Nightlife 娱乐节目

China's entertainment options are improving rapidly. Bars, discos and karaoke parlours are springing up in all the major cities and more cultural events are being held.

What's there to do in the evenings?
wǎnshang yǒu shénme yùlè jiémù?
晚上有什么娱乐节目

Is there a disco here?
zhèr yǒu dísīkē ma?
这儿有迪斯科吗?

Can I buy a tape of this music?

wǒ néng mǎi zhèige yīnyuède lùyīndài ma?

我能买这个音乐的
录音带吗？

I would like to see ...	*wǒ xiǎng kàn ...*	我想看...
an acrobatic troupe	*zájìtuán*	杂技团
a local opera	*dìfāngxì*	地方戏
a movie	*diànyǐng*	电影
Peking opera	*jīngjù*	京剧
a song and dance troupe	*gēwǔtuán*	歌舞团

I would like to reserve tickets for ... show.	*wǒ xiǎng dìng ... piào*	我想订...票
this evening's	*jīntiān wǎnshangde*	今天晚上的
tomorrow evening's	*míngtiān wǎnshangde*	明天晚上的
cinema	*diànyǐngyuàn*	电影院
concert	*yīnyuèhuì*	音乐会
disco	*dísīkē*	迪斯科
theatre	*jùchǎng*	剧场

AROUND TOWN

In the Country

郊遊

China has opened up tremendously since the early '80s but some places in the countryside remain off limits, mainly because they lack any accommodation for foreigners. In spite of this you'll still have plenty of opportunities to get a taste of Chinese country life while you're travelling in China. Bus journeys often break their passage in small country villages, and some of China's most interesting destinations are surrounded by countryside and villages that can be explored on bicycles.

Weather

天气

What's the weather like?
tiānqi zěnmeyàng?

天气怎么样？

It's humid.	*hěn mènrè*	很闷热
It's hot.	*hěn rè*	很热
It's cold.	*hěn lěng*	很冷
It's raining.	*xià yǔ*	下雨
It's windy.	*gūa fēng*	刮风

The weather is nice today.
jīntiānde tiānqi hěn hǎo

今天的天气很好

72

Will it rain tomorrow?
míngtiān huì xià yǔ ma?

明天会下雨吗？

Will it be very cold?
huìbuhuì hěn lěng?

会不会很冷？

cloud	*yún*	云
earth	*tǔ*	土
ice	*bīng*	冰
mud	*wūní*	污泥
rain	*yǔ*	雨
rainy season	*yǔjì*	雨季
snow	*xuě*	雪
sun	*tàiyang*	太阳
weather	*tiānqi*	天气
wind	*fēng*	风

Seasons

季节

spring	*chūntiān*	春天
summer	*xiàtiān*	夏天
autumn	*qiūtiān*	秋天
winter	*dōngtiān*	冬天

Geographical Terms

应用词汇

agriculture	*nóngyè*	农业
beach	*hǎitān*	海滩
cave	*dòng*	洞
city	*chéngshì*	城市
country person (lit: peasant)	*nóngmín*	农民
desert	*shāmò*	沙漠
earthquake	*dìzhèn*	地震

IN THE COUNTRY

farm	*nóngchǎng*	农场
forest	*sēnlín*	森林
grassy plains	*cǎoyuán*	草原
harbour	*gǎng*	港
hill	*xiǎoshān*	小山
hot spring	*wēnquán*	温泉
island	*dǎo*	岛

jungle	*cónglín*	丛林
lake	*hú*	湖
landslide	*shānbēng*	山崩
mountain	*shān*	山
mountain range	*shānmài*	山脉
national park	*guójiā gōngyuán*	国家公园
ocean	*hǎiyáng*	海洋
river	*hé*	河
valley	*xīgǔ*	溪谷
village	*cūnzhuāng*	村庄
waterfall	*pùbù*	瀑布

Animals, Birds & Insects   动物虫鸟

bird	*niǎo*	鸟
butterfly	*húdié*	蝴蝶
camel	*luòtuo*	骆驼
cat	*māo*	猫
chicken	*jī*	鸡
cockroach	*zhāngláng*	蟑螂
cow	*niú*	牛
crocodile	*èyú*	鳄鱼
dog	*gǒu*	狗
donkey	*lú*	驴
fish	*yú*	鱼
fly	*cāngying*	苍蝇

frog	qīngwā	青蛙
goat	shānyáng	山羊
horse	mǎ	马
lizard	xīyì	蜥蜴
monkey	hóuzi	猴子
mosquito	wénzi	蚊子
ox	gōngniú	公牛
panda	xióngmāo	熊猫
pig	zhū	猪
rooster	gōngjī	公鸡
sheep	yáng	羊
snake	shé	蛇
spider	zhīzhū	蜘蛛
turtle	guī	龟
wild animal	yěshòu	野兽

IN THE COUNTRY

Food

饮食

When it's served in banquets or in high-class restaurants, Chinese cuisine is without a doubt among the finest in the world. The long tradition of elevating cookery to an art form means that the modern Chinese are heirs to an astoundingly extensive range of cooking styles. Unfortunately for the traveller in China (and for the Chinese themselves) the meals that grace high-class restaurant tables in Hong Kong bear little resemblance to the simple fare of restaurants in the People's Republic.

If you're watching every cent, it's likely that your diet will consist almost entirely of soup, noodles, rice and stir-fried vegetables but it's worth checking the menus of some hotel or privately run restaurants.

restaurant	*fànguǎn*	饭馆
breakfast	*zǎofàn*	早饭
lunch	*wǔfàn*	午饭
dinner	*wǎnfàn*	晚饭
to eat	*chī*	吃
to drink	*hē*	喝

Etiquette 礼仪

The Chinese have a word for the atmosphere of their restaurants:
rènao. Literally it means 'hot and noisy', and that's the way the
Chinese like it. When the Chinese eat out they like to have *fun* –
the Western style of whispering couples sipping expensive wine
by candlelight is definitely not for them.

There are a few do's and don't's, particularly when you're
eating with Chinese. Perhaps most important, let others pour your
drinks and keep an eye on theirs to make sure they stay topped
up – helping yourself is a sign that your hosts or companions
aren't looking after you properly.

Breakfast 早饭

As in other parts of Asia, the difficult meal for foreigners is
breakfast. The Chinese don't seem to understand the Western
notion of eating light in the morning.

dòujiāng 豆浆
    sweet soya bean milk
yóutiáo 油条
    fried bread stick, similar to a donut and eaten with *dòujiāng*
xīfàn or zhōu 稀饭/粥
    rice porridge
pàocài 泡菜
    pickled vegetables eaten with *xīfàn*

FOOD

bāozi 包子
  steamed buns with different fillings
dòushābāo 豆沙包
  steamed bean-paste bun (sweet)
shāobǐng 烧饼
  sesame seed pancake
tāngmiàn 汤面
  noodle soup

Lunch 午饭

In general, most of the things that are available at dinner time can also be eaten for lunch, but the latter tends to be a more restrained affair than the all-out assault on the digestive tracts that takes place in the evening. Many Chinese take lunch at a *xiǎochīdiàn*, or snack shop. The food in these places is usually cheap and tasty and comes in small serves. The following are some of the more common snacks you'll come across.

mántou 馒头
  plain steamed bun, a common staple in northern China
huājuǎn 花卷
  steamed roll, similar to *mántou*
shuǐjiǎo 水饺
  boiled dumplings usually filled with pork and/or vegetables
zhēngjiǎo 蒸饺
  like *shuǐjiǎo*, only steamed
guōtiē 锅贴
  fried *shuǐjiǎo*
chāshāobāo 叉烧包
  steamed rolls filled with barbecued pork (southern China)

FOOD

húntun 馄饨
  small meat dumplings that come in a soup (known in the West as wonton)
xiǎolóngbāo 小笼包
  small steamed dumplings usually filled with pork
cōngyóubǐng 葱油饼
  a small spring onion-flavoured chepati fried in oil

Dinner 晚饭

This is where the Chinese roll out the big guns. The range of dishes available in China is far too extensive to list here. There are many regional differences. In the north, for example, steamed breads, not rice, are the staple; inhabitants of the coastal regions of Jiangsu, Shanghai and Zhejiang are renowned for their sweet tooth, use rice as a staple, and have a cuisine that includes plenty of seafood dishes; in the south, Cantonese cuisine is the style of Chinese cooking that most Westerners will have already come across, with its famous exports like sweet and sour, and yum cha (dim sum); western China, in particular Sichuan, is famous for its use of chillis and peppers.

The following list comprises the more well-known dishes to be found in China. If there is any dish that takes your fancy, keep pointing to it in the

FOOD

book every time you eat out – sooner or later you're going to hit a restaurant that has it on the menu.

Poultry

běijīng kǎoyā 北京烤鸭
Peking duck (difficult to get outside Beijing)

xiāngsū yā/jī 香酥鸭/鸡
crispy fried duck/chicken

gōngbǎo jīdīng 宫保鸡丁
a popular Sichuan dish; chicken stir fried with peanuts and chillis

jiàohuà jī 叫化鸡
known as 'beggar's chicken', the chicken is marinated, wrapped in bamboo leaves and then roasted

guàiwèi jī 怪味鸡
the name literally means 'strange-tasting chicken'; in actual fact there's nothing strange about this chicken prepared with a delicious pepper and sesame paste sauce

jiàngbào jīdīng 酱爆鸡丁
marinated chicken breast, stir fried in a special sauce

Pork

Pork is the meat most frequently eaten by the Chinese. Usually, if the name of the meat in a dish is not specified, it is pork.

huíguō ròu 回锅肉
  literally 'return-to-the-pot meat', this is a spicy dish where the pork is first boiled and then stir fried

gǔlǎo ròu 古老肉
  sweet-and-sour pork

tángcù páigǔ 糖醋排骨
  sweet-and-sour spare ribs

hóngshāo ròu 红烧肉
  'red-cooked meat'; a kind of stew made with a lightly sweetened dark soya sauce stock

yúxiāng ròusī 鱼香肉丝
  literally 'fish-flavoured meat'; the rich flavour is produced by stir frying shredded pork with a liberal dollop of garlic, ginger and chillis

gōngbǎo ròudīng 宫保肉丁
  shredded pork stir fried with chillis and peanuts; invented by the poet Su Dongpo

mùěr ròu 木耳肉
  shredded pork stir fried with wood ears (a kind of mushroom)

jiàngbào ròusī 酱爆肉丝
  marinated pork cooked in a special sauce

làzǐ ròudīng 辣子肉丁
  diced pork with chillis

dōngpō mēnròu 东坡闷肉
  invented by the poet Dong Po, pork fillet is marinated, boiled and steamed until it's as tender as bean curd

báiqiē ròu 白切肉
  boiled pork eaten cold with various dips

shīzi tóu 狮子头
  literally 'lion's head'; meatballs with cabbage

FOOD

Seafood 海味

The word for fish, *yú*, also means plenty or surplus, and is traditionally given pride of place in celebratory banquets and in feasts laid out for guests. If you're lucky enough to be invited to a Chinese home for a meal, it's likely that your hosts will pick sparingly at the seafood while dolloping great spoonfuls into your bowl. One way to make sure they eat some too is to reciprocate by loading up their bowl.

qīngzhēng yú　清蒸鱼
　　steamed fish; the fish is usually steamed in a marinade of soya sauce, garlic and spring onions
tángcù yú　糖醋鱼
　　sweet-and-sour fish
hóngshāo yú　红烧鱼
　　red-cooked fish; the fish is braised in a soya sauce stock
gānshāo yú　干烧鱼
　　fish braised with chillis and bean sauce

FOOD

Vegetables

Simple vegetable dishes, like Chinese cabbage stir fried with garlic and soya sauce, are very popular with the Chinese and are considered a good accompaniment to meat dishes. Vegetarians travelling around China should always be able to find a restaurant that is able to prepare one of the following dishes.

chǎo shíjǐn shūcài　炒什锦蔬菜
　　stir-fried mixed vegetables
shāo èr dōng　烧二冬
　　mushrooms and vegetables stir fried together
xiānmǐ càihuā　鲜米菜花
　　mushrooms and cauliflower stir fried together
chǎo gānlán　炒芥蓝
　　stir-fried broccoli
shāo qiézi　烧茄子
　　braised eggplant
hóngshāo dòufu　红烧豆腐
　　red-cooked bean curd

Soup

Unlike Westerners, the Chinese generally have soup at the end of the meal. With Peking duck for example, it is customary for the meal to close with duck soup made from the bones of the duck. In many cases Chinese soups will seem thin and a little bland to Westerners, as they are often nothing more than a lightly seasoned stock.

miàntāng　面汤
　　noodle soup
jī tāng　鸡汤
　　chicken soup

FOOD

jīdàn tāng 鸡蛋汤
  egg-drop soup
zhàcài tāng 榨菜汤
  pickled vegetable soup
suānlà tāng 酸辣汤
  hot-and-sour soup
xīhóngshì jīdàn tāng 西红柿鸡蛋汤
  egg and tomato soup

Dessert
básī píngguǒ 拔丝苹果
  apple dipped first into hot caramel and then into iced water
bābǎo fàn 八宝饭
  eight-treasure rice
xìngrénsū 杏仁酥
  almond biscuit
xìngrén dòufu 杏仁豆腐
  almond bean curd
dòufu hūa 豆腐花
  soft bean curd with ginger-flavoured sweetened water

zǎoní bǐng 枣泥饼
  date-filled biscuits
yuè bǐng 月饼
  lotus-paste cakes eaten at the mid-Autumn festival

FOOD

At the Restaurant

饭馆服务

A table for ... please.

   ... wèi

...位

Waiter!

   fúwùyuán!

服务员!

Can I see the menu, please?

   qǐng gěi wǒ kànkàn càidān

请给我看看菜单

Do you have an English menu?

   nǐ yǒu yīngwén càidān ma?

你有英文菜单吗?

What is this/that?

   zhè/nà shi shénme?

这/那是什么?

Can you recommend any dishes?

   nǐ néng jièshao shénme cài ma?

你能介绍什么菜吗?

Another one, please!

   qǐng zài lái yíge!

请再来一个

I would like ...

   wǒ yào ...

我要...

I'm hungry.

   wǒ èle

我饿了

I'm thirsty.

   wǒ kěle

我渴了

Not too spicy, please.

   qǐng búyào tài là

请不要太辣

No monosodium glutimate, please.

   qǐng búyào fàng wèijīng

请不要放味精

Please give me a knife and fork.

   qǐng gěi wǒ chāzi hé dāozi

请给我叉子和刀子

FOOD

This isn't what I ordered.
zhè búshì wǒ diǎnde cài　　　这不是我点的菜
The meal was delicious.
hǎochī jíle　　　好吃极了
I'm full.
wǒ chībǎole　　　我吃饱了
The bill please.
qǐng jiézhàng　　　请结帐

Vegetarian

Even though the Chinese have a term for vegetarians, it's almost unheard of for a Chinese person to adopt a vegetarian diet except by necessity. Some Western travellers claim that the only way to make the Chinese understand that you are a strict vegetarian (and not keen on eating 'vegetable dishes' that have simply had most of the meat picked out of them) is to tell them that you're Buddhist.

I am vegetarian.
wǒ shi chīsùde　　　我是吃素的
I don't eat meat.
wǒ bù chī ròu　　　我不吃肉
I don't eat fish.
wǒ bù chī yú　　　我不吃鱼
I am Buddhist.
wǒ xìn fójiào　　　我信佛教

Chinese Regional Cuisines

Beijing food	*běijīngcài*	京菜
Cantonese food	*guǎngdōngcài/yuècài*	广东菜/粤菜
Chaozhou food	*cháozhōucài*	潮州菜

FOOD

Chinese food	zhōngcān	中餐
Eastern Chinese food	huáiyángcài	淮扬菜
Hunan food	xiāngcài	湘菜
Kejia food	dōngjiāngcài/kèjiācài	东江菜/客家菜
Northern Chinese food	běifāngcài	北方菜
Shandong food	shāndōngcài	山东菜
Shanghai food	shànghǎicài	上海菜
Sichuan food	chuāncài	川菜
Taiwanese food	táiwāncài	台湾菜

Other National Cuisines

fast food	kuàicān	快餐
French food	fǎguócài	法国菜
Indian food	yìndùcài	印度菜
Japanese food	rìběnliàolǐ	日本料理
Japanese tep-penyaki	rìběntiěbǎnshāo	日本铁板烧
Korean food	hánguóvài	韩国菜
Thai food	tàiguócài	泰国菜
South-East Asian food	nányángcài	南洋菜
Vietnamese food	yuènáncài	越南菜
Western food	xīcān	西餐

Meat 肉类

beef	niúròu	牛肉
chicken	jī	鸡
duck	yā	鸭
ham	huǒtuǐ	火腿

liver	*gān*	肝
mutton	*yángròu*	羊肉
pork	*zhūròu*	猪肉
sausage	*xiāngcháng*	香肠
tripe	*niúdù*	牛肚

Seafood 海鲜

abalone	*bàoyú*	鲍鱼
bream	*biānyú*	鳊鱼
carp	*lǐyú*	鲤鱼
crab	*pángxie*	螃蟹
eel	*mànyú*	鳗鱼
fish	*yú*	鱼
lobster	*lóngxiā*	龙虾
mandarin fish	*guìyú*	鳜鱼
perch	*lúyú*	鲈鱼
prawns	*xiā*	虾
seafood	*hǎixiā*	海鲜
shark's fin	*yúchì*	鱼翅
squid	*yóuyú*	鱿鱼
sturgeon	*huángyú*	鳇鱼
yellow croaker	*dà huángyú*	大黄鱼

Vegetables 蔬菜

bamboo shoots	*zhúsǔn*	竹笋
beans	*dòu*	豆
chilli	*làjiāo*	辣椒
Chinese cabbage	*báicài*	白菜
cucumber	*huánggūa*	黄瓜
eggplant	*qiézi*	茄子
garlic	*suàn*	蒜

FOOD

ginger	*jiāng*	姜
mushroom	*mógu*	蘑菇
potato	*tǔdòu*	土豆
spring onion	*cōng*	葱
tomato	*xìhóngshì*	西红柿
vegetable	*shūcài*	蔬菜

Fruit 水果

apple	*píngguǒ*	苹果
apricot	*xìng*	杏
banana	*xiāngjiāo*	香蕉
cherries	*yīngtáo*	樱桃
Chinese dates	*zǎo*	枣
coconut	*yēzi*	椰子
grapes	*pútao*	葡萄
lemon	*níngméng*	柠檬
loquat	*pípa*	枇杷
lychees	*lìzhī*	荔枝
mango	*mángguǒ*	芒果
orange	*júzi*	桔子
pear	*lí*	梨
peach	*táozi*	桃子
plum	*lǐzi*	李子
sweet melon	*tiángūa*	甜瓜
tangerine	*gānjú*	柑橘
watermelon	*xīgūa*	西瓜

FOOD

Dairy Products　　　　　　　　　　　　乳制品

With the exception of yoghurt, which is eaten in western China,
dairy products are a rarity. The Chinese do not use them at all in
their cooking and associate the drinking of milk and so on with
the diet of babies, not of adults.

butter	*huángyóu*	黄油
cheese	*nǎilào*	奶酪
cream	*nǎiyóu*	奶油
ice cream	*bīngqílín*	冰淇淋
milk	*niúnǎi*	牛奶
yoghurt	*suānnǎi*	酸奶

Condiments　　　　　　　　　　　　　调味料

chilli	*làjiāo*	辣椒
chilli sauce	*làjiàng*	辣酱
cinnamon	*guìpí*	桂皮
cloves	*dīngxiāng*	丁香
garlic	*suàn*	蒜
ginger	*jiāng*	姜
MSG (monosodium glutimate)	*wèijīng*	味精
salt	*yán*	盐
soy sauce	*jiàngyóu*	酱油
star aniseed	*dàliào*	大料
sugar	*táng*	糖
vinegar	*cù*	醋

Other Food 杂粮

beancurd	*dòufu*	豆腐
biscuits	*bǐnggān*	饼干
bread	*miànbāo*	面包
steamed buns	*bāozi*	包子
cake	*dàngāo*	蛋糕
congee	*xīfànzhōu*	稀饭/粥
dessert	*tiánpǐn*	甜品
dumplings	*jiǎozi*	饺子
egg	*jīdàn*	鸡蛋
cold hors d'oeuvre	*lěng pánr*	冷盘儿
noodles	*miàntiáo*	面条
rice noodles	*mǐxiànmǐfěn*	米线/米粉
noodles in soup	*tāngmiàn*	面汤
noodles (fried)	*chǎomiàn*	炒面
pastry	*gāodiǎn*	糕点
rice	*dàmǐ/mǐfàn*	大米/米饭
plain rice	*báimǐfàn*	白米饭
fried rice	*chǎofàn*	炒饭
soup	*tāng*	汤
toast	*kǎo miànbāo*	烤面包

Cooking Methods 烹调方法

barbecued	*tànhuǒkǎo*	炭火烤
braised	*gānshāo*	干烧
deep-fried	*jiāozhá*	焦炸
fried	*zhá*	炸
roasted	*kǎo*	烤
stir-fried	*bàochǎo*	爆炒
steamed	*qīngzhēng*	清蒸

FOOD

Drinks 饮料

During meals the most popular drink among the Chinese would have to be Chinese tea. The Chinese seldom drink alcohol with a meal, though if you are lucky enough to be invited to a banquet you will be expected to join in the toasts with *máotái*, a powerful spirit that makes an excellent substitute for metholated spirits. In most restaurants it is possible to order beer.

Alcoholic Drinks

beer	*píjiǔ*	啤酒
spirits	*báijiǔ*	白酒
whisky	*wēishìjì*	威士忌
wine	*pútáojiǔ*	葡萄酒

When you're drinking with the Chinese, the usual toast literally means 'dry glass'. It's generally only used when you intend to finish the glass off in one gulp.

Cheers!　　　　　*gānbēi!*　　　干杯!

Non-Alcoholic Drinks

apple juice	*píngguǒzhī*	苹果汁
boiled water	*kāishuǐ*	开水
fizzy drink	*qìshuǐ*	汽水
fruit juice	*guǒzhī*	果汁
lemonade	*níngméng qìshuǐ*	柠檬汽水
milk	*niúnǎi*	牛奶
mineral water	*kuàngquánshuǐ*	矿泉水
orange juice	*júzishuǐ*	桔子水
water	*shuǐ*	水

Hot Drinks

The Chinese are not coffee drinkers, and outside the main cities you're unlikely to come across anywhere serving coffee. One way of coping with this is to have a go at starving the coffee addiction by turning to China's delicious teas. These teas are enjoyed not only for their taste but also for their medicinal qualities.

coffee	*kāfēi*	咖啡
black	*chúnde*	纯的
with milk	*jiā niúnǎide*	加牛奶的
green tea	*lǜchá*	绿茶
jasmine tea	*mòlìhuāchá*	茉莉花茶
oolong tea	*wūlóngchá*	乌龙茶

Some Useful Words 应用词汇

ashtray	*yānhuīgāng*	烟灰缸
bowl	*wǎn*	碗
chopsticks	*kuàizi*	筷子
cold	*lěng*	冷
cup	*bēizi*	杯子

fork	*chāzi*	叉子
hot	*rè*	热
knife	*dāozi*	刀子
plate	*pán*	盘
restaurant	*cāntīng/fànguǎn*	餐厅，饭馆
snack	*xiǎochī/diǎnxīn*	小吃，点心
spoon	*sháozi*	勺子
table	*zhūozi*	桌子
toothpick	*yáqiān*	牙签

Shopping

购物

Department stores now sell imported goods, once the domain of the Friendship Stores. Only the large Friendship Stores in Beijing, Shanghai and Canton are in a class of their own for their extraordinary range of goods. Imported goods will have quite a high mark-up. If there's anything, like coffee or photographic film, that you absolutely can't do without, it's a good idea to bring it with you. As in other Asian countries, China has plenty of markets.

Where can I buy ...?
wǒ zài nǎr néng mǎi ...?   我在哪儿能买...?
Where is ...?
... zài nǎr?   ...在哪儿?

Where is the nearest ...?	*lí zhèr zuìjìnde ... zài nǎr?*	离这儿最近的... 在哪儿?
antique shop	*gǔdǒngdiàn*	古董店
baker's	*miànbāodiàn*	面包店
bank	*yínháng*	银行
bookshop	*shūdiàn*	书店
camera shop	*zhàoxiàng qìcái shāngdiàn*	照相器材商店

department store	*bǎihuò shāngdiàn*	百货商店
free market	*zìyóu shìchǎng*	自由市场
friendship store	*yǒuyì shāngdiàn*	友谊商店
laundry	*xǐyīdiàn*	洗衣店
market	*shìchǎng*	市场
pharmacy	*yàodiàn*	药店
shop	*shāngdiàn*	商店
shopping centre	*shāngchǎng*	商场
shoe shop	*xiédiàn*	鞋店
souvenir shop	*lù yóu jìniànpǐn shāngdiàn*	旅游纪念品商店
tailor's	*cáifengdiàn*	裁缝店
vegetable shop	*shūcàidiàn*	蔬菜店

Making a Purchase   服务

I'd like to buy ...
  wǒ xiǎng mǎi ...

我想买...

I'm just looking.
  wǒ xiān kànkan

我先看看

How much does this cost?
  zhèige dūoshao qián?

这个多少钱？

Can you help me?
  nǐ néng bāngzhù wǒ ma?

你能帮助我吗？

Miss!
  xiǎojiě!

小姐！

Sir!
  shīfu!

师父！

Excuse me, could you come
here and help me, please?
  duìbuqǐ, máfan nǐ lái zhèr bāngzhù wǒ?

对不起，麻烦你来这儿帮助我

SHOPPING

Bargaining

折扣

The government-run stores are almost always subjected to fixed prices, and bargaining is unlikely to get you anywhere. On the streets, however, bargaining skills can come in handy. Don't get too carried away though; the Chinese may feel insulted if you try to undercut their original asking price by too much.

Can you reduce the price?
néng piányì yìdiǎnr ma?

能便宜一点儿吗?

Do you give a discount?
néng dǎ zhékòu ma?

能打折扣吗?

It's too expensive.
tài guìle

太贵了

I'll give you ... yuan.
wǒ gěi nǐ ... kuài

我给你...块

Souvenirs 纪念品

Please show me some ...	*qǐng gěi wǒ kànyikan ...*	请给我看一看...
calligraphy	*shūfǎ*	书法
carpets	*dìtǎn*	地毯
chinaware	*cíqì*	瓷器
chopsticks	*kuàizi*	筷子
earrings	*ěrhuán*	耳环
embroidery	*xiùhūa zhìpǐn*	绣花制品
fabrics	*bùliào*	布料
fans	*shànzi*	扇子
furniture	*jiājù*	家具
jade products	*yùshí zhìpǐn*	玉石制品
jewellery	*zhūbǎo shǒushì*	珠宝首饰
lacquerware	*qīqì*	漆器
musical instruments	*yuèqì*	乐器
paintings	*huà*	画
paper cuts	*jiǎnzhǐ*	剪纸
porcelain	*cíqì*	瓷器
pottery	*táoqì*	陶器

| scrolls | *juànzhóu* | 卷轴 |
| silk products | *sīzhīpǐn* | 丝织品 |

衣服

Clothing

blouse	*nǚchènshān*	女衬衫
bra	*rǔzhào*	乳罩
cap	*màozi*	帽子
clothing	*yīfu*	衣服
coat	*dàyī*	大衣
dress	*liányīqún*	连衣裙
dressing gown	*yùyī*	浴衣
gloves	*shǒutào*	手套
hat	*lǐmào*	礼帽
jacket	*shàngyī*	上衣
jeans	*niúzǎikù*	牛仔裤
jumper	*máoyī*	毛衣
pyjamas	*shuìyī*	睡衣
raincoat	*yǔyī*	雨衣

sandals	*liángxié*	凉鞋
scarf	*wéijīn*	围巾
shirt	*chènshān*	衬衫
shoes	*xié*	鞋
shorts	*duǎnkù*	短裤
skirt	*qúnzi*	裙子
socks	*wàzi*	袜子
stockings	*chángwà*	长袜
suit	*xīfú*	西服
swimming suit	*yóuyǒngyī*	游泳衣
trousers	*chángkù*	长裤
T-shirt	*zhēnzhī chènshān*	针织衬衫
underpants	*nèikù*	内裤

I would like something like this.
  wǒ yào yíjiàn xiàng zhèige yàngzide
  我要一件像这个样子的

Can you show me another one?
  kěyǐ zài gěi wǒ kànyikan biéde ma?
  可以再给我看一看别的吗?

Can I try it on?
  wǒ kěyǐ shìchuān yíxià ma?
  我可以试穿一下吗?

Is there a mirror?
zhèr yǒu jìngzi ma?　　　　　　　　这儿有镜子吗?

It fits well.
hěn héshì　　　　　　　　　　　很合适

It doesn't fit.
bù héshì　　　　　　　　　　　不合适

It's too ...	*tài ...*	太...
big	*dàle*	大了
small	*xiǎole*	小了
long	*chángle*	长了
short	*duǎnle*	短了
loose	*féile*	肥了
tight	*jǐnle*	紧了

Can it be altered?
néngbunéng gǎi yíxià?　　　　　　能不能改一下?

Materials

cotton	*miánbù*	棉布
handmade	*shǒugōngzhìde*	手工制的
leather	*pígé*	皮子
linen	*yàmábù*	亚麻布
satin	*duànzi*	缎子
silk	*sīchóu*	丝绸
wool	*chúnmáo*	纯毛

Colours

black	*hēisè*	黑色
blue	*lánsè*	蓝色
brown	*hèsè*	褐色
dark	*shēn*	深

golden	*jīnhuángsè*	金黄色
green	*lǜsè*	绿色
grey	*hūsè*	灰色
light	*qiǎn*	浅
orange	*júhóngsè*	桔红色
pink	*fěnhóngsè*	粉红色
purple	*zǐsè*	紫色
red	*hóngsè*	红色
white	*báisè*	白色
yellow	*huángsè*	黄色

Stationery & Books   文具报刊

book	*shū*	书
dictionary	*zìdiǎn*	字典
drawing paper	*túhuà zhǐ*	图画纸
exercise book	*liànxíběn*	练习本
envelope/s	*xìnfēng*	信封
eraser	*xiàngpí*	橡皮
magazine	*zázhì*	杂志
map	*dìtú*	地图
newspaper	*bàozhǐ*	报纸
newspaper in English	*yīngwén bàozhǐ*	英文报纸
notebook	*běnzi*	本子
novel	*xiǎoshūo*	小说
novels in English	*yīngwén xiǎoshūo*	英文小说
pen (ballpoint)	*yuánzhūbǐ*	圆珠笔
pencil	*qiānbǐ*	铅笔
scissors	*jiǎndāo*	剪刀
writing paper	*xìnzhǐ*	信纸

Photography 照相

Take all the photographic equipment you need with you to China; although the Chinese are enthusiastic photographers there is little in the way of photographic equipment for sale anywhere. Even film, especially slide film, is reasonably expensive to buy and process. If your camera uses batteries, be sure to take spares.

I'd like a film for this camera.
wǒ xiǎngyào yìjuǎn shìyú   我想要一卷适于这种
zhèizhǒng zhàoxiàngjīde   照相机的胶卷
jiāojuǎn

How much do you charge for processing?
chōngxǐ zhèijuǎn jiāojuǎn   冲洗这卷胶卷多少钱?
duōshao qián?

When will the pictures be ready?
shénme shíhou chōngxǐ hǎo?   什么时候冲洗好?

Can you fix cameras?
nǐmen xiū zhàoxiàngjī ma?   你们修照相机吗?

B&W	*hēibáide*	黑白的
camera	*zhàoxiàngjī*	照相机
colour	*cǎisède*	彩色的
colour slide	*cǎisè huàndēngpiàn*	彩色幻灯片
film	*jiāojuǎn*	胶卷
flash	*shǎnguāngdēng*	闪光灯
lens	*jìngtóu*	镜头
lens cap	*jìngtóugài*	镜头盖
light metre	*cèguāngbiǎo*	测光表

Smoking　　　　　　　　　　　　香烟

a carton	*yìtiáo*	一条
cigarettes	*xiāngyān*	香烟
lighter	*dǎhuǒjī*	打火机
matches	*huǒchái*	火柴
pipe	*yāndǒu*	烟斗

No Smoking.
　bùzhǔnxīyān　　　　　　　　　不准吸烟

A packet of cigarettes, please.
　qǐng gěi wǒ yìbāo xiāngyān　请给我一包香烟

Do you mind if I smoke?
　wǒxīyān nǐjièyìma?　　　　　我吸烟你介意吗？

Do you have a light?
　yǒu huǒchái ma?　　　　　　有火柴吗？

I don't smoke.
　wǒbuhuìxīyān　　　　　　　　我不会吸烟

Please don't smoke
　qǐngbúyàoxīyān　　　　　　　请不要吸烟

I'm trying to give up.
　wǒzhèngzàijièyān　　　　　　我正在戒烟

Weights & Measures　　　重量长度

milligram	*háokè*	毫克
gram	*kè*	克
kilogram	*gōngjīn*	公斤
millimetre	*háomǐ*	毫米
centimetre	*límǐ*	厘米
metre	*mǐ*	米
kilometre	*gōnglǐ*	公里
litre	*shēng*	升

Sizes & Quantities   大小数量

small	*xiǎo*	小
smaller	*gèng xiǎo*	更小
smallest	*zuì xiǎo*	最小
big	*dà*	大
bigger	*gèng dà*	更大
biggest	*zuì dà*	最大
heavy	*zhòng*	重
light	*qīng*	轻
more	*dūo*	多
less	*shǎo*	少
too much/many	*tài dūo*	太多
many	*hěn dūo*	很多
long	*cháng*	长
short	*duǎn*	短
tall	*gāo*	高
enough	*gòu*	够
a little bit	*yìdiǎnr*	一点儿

Some Useful Phrases   应用词句

Do you have others?
  nǐ yǒu biéde ma?   你有别的吗?
I don't like it.
  wǒ bùxǐhuan   我不喜欢
I'd prefer something of better
quality.
  wǒ bǐjiào xǐhuan zhìliang hǎo   我比较喜欢质量好
  yìdiǎnrde   一点儿的
Can I see it?
  néng kànyikan ma?   能看一看吗?

I'll take (buy) it.
   wǒ jiù mǎi zhèige

我就买这个

There is none.
   méiyǒu

没有

Which one?
   něige?

哪个?

Show it to me.
   gěi wo kànyikan

给我看一看

Can you write down the price?
   nǐ néngbunéng bǎ jiàqián xiěxiàlai?

你能不能把价钱
写下来?

Do you accept credit cards?
   néng yòng xìnyòngkǎ fùkuǎn ma?

能用信用卡付款吗?

Please wrap it for me.
   qǐng gěi wǒ bāo yíxià

请给我包一下

Some Useful Words 应用词汇

backpack	*bèibāo*	背包
handbag	*shǒutíbāo*	手提包
battery	*diànchí*	电池
bottle	*píng*	瓶
box	*hé*	盒
button (clothes)	*niǔkòu*	钮扣
candle	*làzhú*	蜡烛
discount	*zhékòu*	折扣
gold	*jīn*	金
mirror	*jìngzi*	镜子
receipt	*shōujù*	收据
silver	*yín*	银

Health

健康

Doctors in China are just as likely to draw on Chinese traditional medicine as on Western medicine, and in large hospitals treatment will probably be a combination of both these approaches. In the big cities like Beijing and Shanghai, where there are sizeable foreign populations, medical services are available with English-speaking doctors. Elsewhere, the chances of finding an English-speaking doctor are more remote. Medical services are generally very cheap, although random foreigner surcharges may apply

I am sick.
wǒ shēngbìngle   我生病了
My friend is sick.
wǒde péngyou shēngbìngle   我的朋友生病了
I need a doctor.
wǒ děi jiàn dàifu   我得见大夫
Is there a doctor who speaks
English here?
*zhèr yǒu huì jiǎng yīngyǔde
dàifu ma?*   这儿有会讲英语的
                                             大夫吗?
Can you get me a doctor?
qǐng zhǎo yíwèi dàifu?   请找一位大夫

Where is ...?	... zài nǎr?	...在哪儿?
a doctor	dàifu	大夫
the hospital	yīyuàn	医院
the chemist	yàodiàn	药店

Complaints　　　　　　　　　　　　　　病状

I feel dizzy.
  wǒ tóuyūn　　　　　　　　　　我头晕

I feel weak.
  wǒ gǎndào shuāiruòwúlì　　　　我感到衰弱无力

I feel tired all over.
  wǒ húnshēn méijìn　　　　　　我浑身没劲

I've been bitten by an insect.
  wǒ bèi shénme chóngzi yǎole　　我被什么虫子咬了

I have trouble breathing.
  wǒ hūxī kùnnan　　　　　　　我呼吸困难

I have a heart condition.
  wo yǒu xīnzàngbìng　　　　　　我有心脏病

I've been vomiting.
  wǒ yìzhí tù　　　　　　　　　我一直吐

I can't sleep.
  wǒ shuìbuzháo　　　　　　　　我睡不着

I can't move my ...
  wǒde ... dòngbuliao　　　　　　我的...动不了

It hurts here.
zhèr téng   这儿疼
My ... hurts.
wǒde ... téng   我的...疼

I have ...   *wǒ ...*   我...
  altitude   *yǒu gāoshānbìng*   有高山病
    sickness
  asthma   *xiàochuǎn*   哮喘
  a burn   *shāoshāngle*   烧伤了
  constipation   *biànmì*   便秘
  a cold   *shāngfēngle*   伤风了
  a cough   *késou*   咳嗽
  the cramps   *chōujīnle*   抽筋了
  diabetes   *yǒu tángniào bìng*   有糖尿病
  diarrhoea   *xièdùzi*   泻肚子
  dysentery   *yǒu lìji*   有痢疾
  epilepsy   *diānxián*   癫痫
  a fever   *fāshāole*   发烧了
  food poisoning   *shíwù zhòngdúle*   食物中毒了
  headache   *tóuténg*   头疼
  hepatitis   *déle gānyán*   得了肝炎
  indigestion   *xiāohuà bùliáng*   消化不良
  an infection   *fāyánle*   发炎了
  influenza   *gǎnmàole*   感冒了
  an itch   *yǎng*   痒
  lice   *yǒu shīzi*   有虱了
  low/high blood   *xuěyā*   血压过低/过高
    pressure   *guòdī/guògāo*
  malaria   *délenǚeji*   得了疟疾

a migraine	*zhōuqīxìng piāntóutòng*	周期性偏头痛
rheumatism	*yǒu fēngshī*	有风湿
a sore throat	*hóulóng téng*	喉咙疼
stomachache	*dùzi téng*	肚子疼
sunstroke	*zhòngshǔle*	中暑了
toothache	*yá téng*	牙疼
typhoid	*yǒu shānghán*	有伤寒
venereal disease	*yǒu xìngbìng*	有性病

It's ...	*zhèr ...*	这儿...
broken	*duànle*	断了
dislocated	*tūojiùle*	脱臼了
sprained	*niǔshāngle*	扭伤了

Women's Health

Could I have a female doctor?
qǐng gěi wǒ zhǎo yíwèi nǚdàifu?　请给我找一位女大夫

I'm on the pill.
wǒ fú bìyùnyào　我服避孕药

I'm pregnant.
wǒ huáiyùnle　我怀孕了

I haven't had my period
for ... months.
wǒ tíngjīng yǒu ... ge yuèle　我停经有...个月了

Allergies

过敏

I'm allergic to ...	*wǒ duì ... guòmǐn*	我对...过敏
antibiotics	*kàngshēngsù*	抗生素
aspirin	*āsīpǐlín*	阿司匹林
penicillin	*qīngméisù*	青霉素

Parts of the Body　　　　　　身体各部

ankle	*jiǎowàn*	脚腕
appendix	*lánwěi*	烂尾
arm	*gēbo*	胳膊
back	*bèi*	背
blood	*xuě*	血
bone	*gǔtou*	骨头
brain	*nǎodai*	脑袋
breast	*rǔfáng*	乳房
chest	*xiōngbù*	胸部
ear	*ěrduo*	耳朵
elbow	*zhǒu*	肘
eye	*yǎnjīng*	眼睛
face	*liǎn*	脸
finger	*shǒuzhǐ*	手指
foot	*jiǎo*	脚
hand	*shǒu*	手
head	*tóu*	头
heart	*xīnzàng*	心脏
hip	*pìgu*	屁股
kidney	*shèn*	肾
knee	*xīgài*	膝盖
leg	*tuǐ*	腿
liver	*gān*	肝
lung	*fèi*	肺
mouth	*zuǐ*	嘴
muscle	*jīròu*	肌肉
neck	*bózi*	脖子
nose	*bízi*	鼻子
rib	*lèigǔ*	肋骨
shoulder	*jiānbǎng*	肩膀

skin	*pífu*	皮肤
spine	*jǐzhūī*	脊椎
stomach	*wèi*	胃
teeth	*yáchǐ*	牙齿
throat	*sǎngzi*	嗓子
tongue	*shétou*	舌头
tonsils	*biǎntáoxiàn*	扁桃腺
wrist	*shǒuwàn*	手腕

At the Chemist　　　　　　药店

You would be wise to bring prescribed drugs with you. Alternatively you could look into Chinese traditional herbal medicine, a form of treatment that is taken very seriously in China.

I need something for
diarrhoea.
  wǒ yào zhì fùxiède yào　　　　　我要治腹泻的药
I need something for a cold.
  wǒ yào zhì gǎnmàode yào　　　我要治感冒的药
Do I need a prescription
for ...?
  ... yīnggāi shi dàifu kāide ma?　　...应该是大夫开的吗?

How many times a day?
měitiān chī jǐcì?   每天吃几次？

aspirin	*āsīpǐlín*	阿司匹林
baby's bottle	*nǎipíng*	奶瓶
Band-Aids	*chuàngkětiē*	创可贴
chlorine tablets	*lǜpiàn*	氯片
comb	*shūzi*	梳子
condom/s	*bìyùntào*	避孕套
deodorant	*chútǐxiùyè*	除体臭液
hairbrush	*fàshūa*	发刷
insect repellant	*chúchóngjì*	除虫剂
iodine	*diǎnjiǔ*	碘酒
laxative	*huǎnxièjì*	缓泻剂
moisturising cream	*rùnfūshūang*	润肤霜
razor	*tìxūdāo*	剃须刀
sanitary napkins	*fùnǚwèishēngjīn*	妇女卫生巾
shampoo	*xǐfàjì*	洗发剂
shaving cream	*tìxū zàoyè*	剃须皂液
soap	*féizào*	肥皂
suntan cream	*shàihēigāo*	晒黑膏
talcum powder	*shuǎngshēnfěn*	爽身粉
tissues	*zhǐ shǒujuàn*	纸手绢
toilet paper	*wèishēngzhǐ*	卫生纸
toothbrush	*yá shūa*	牙刷
toothpaste	*yágāo*	牙膏

At the Dentist   牙医

Is there a good dentist here?
zhèr yǒu hǎo yákē dàifu ma?   这儿有好牙科大夫吗？
I have a toothache.
wǒ yá téng   我牙疼

at the top	zài shàngmian	在上面
at the bottom	zài xiàmian	在下面
at the front	zài qiánmian	在前面
at the back	zài hòumian	在后面

I don't want it extracted.
    qǐng búyào bá   请不要拔

Please give me an anaesthetic.
    qǐng gěi wǒ dǎ máyào   请给我打麻药

Some Useful Words   应用词汇

accident	shìgù	事故
acupuncture	zhēnjiǔ	针灸
antibiotic	kàngshēngsù	抗生素
antiseptic cream	xiāodúgāo	消毒膏
aspirin	āsīpǐlín	阿司匹林
bandage	bēngdài	绷带
bleed	chūxuě	出血
blood pressure	xuěyā	血压
blood test	yànxuě	验血
contraceptive	bìyùnyào	避孕药
faeces	dàbiàn	大便
injection	dǎ zhēn	打针
menstruation	yuèjīng	月经
nauseous	ěxīn	恶心
ointment	ruǎngāo	软膏
oxygen	yǎngqì	氧气
pus	nóng	脓液
urine	niào	脓
vitamin	wéishēngsù	维生素

Time & Dates

日期时间

Telling the Time   时间

Once you've learnt your numbers, telling the time in Chinese is a piece of cake. After the hour place the word *diǎn*, which literally means 'point', then the number of minutes it is past the hour (see Numbers & Amounts, page 124) and then the word *fēn* ('minutes') after. You may hear the word *zhōng,* which tramslates as 'o'clock' in English, placed at the end of all this, but it is optional.

What time is it?
xiànzài jǐdiǎnle?   现在几点了？

9 am	*zǎoshang jiǔdiǎn*	早上九点
12 noon	*zhōngwǔ shíèrdiǎn*	中午十二点
1.10	*yìdiǎn shífēn*	一点十分
2.15	*liǎngdiǎn shíwǔfēn*	二两点十五分
3.20	*sāndiǎn èrshífēn*	三点二十分
4.30	*sìdiǎn bàn*	四点半
5.40	*wǔdiǎn sìshífēn*	五点四十分
6.45	*liùdiǎn sìshíwǔfēn*	六点四十五分
o'clock	*zhōng*	钟
am	*shàngwǔ*	上午
pm	*xiàwǔ*	下午

in the morning	*zǎoshang*	早上
in the afternoon	*xiàwǔ*	下午
in the evening	*wǎnshang*	晚上
hour	*xiǎoshí*	小时
minute	*fēnzhōng*	分钟
second	*miǎozhōng*	秒钟
half an hour	*bàn xiǎoshí*	半小时
quarter of an hour	*yíkè zhōng*	一刻钟

Days 星期

Monday	*xīngqīyī*	星期一
Tuesday	*xīngqīèr*	星期二
Wednesday	*xīngqīsān*	星期三
Thursday	*xīngqīsì*	星期四
Friday	*xīngqīwǔ*	星期五
Saturday	*xīngqīliù*	星期六
Sunday	*xīngqītiān*	星期天

Months 月份

January	*yíyuè*	一月
February	*èryuè*	二月
March	*sānyuè*	三月
April	*sìyuè*	四月
May	*wǔyuè*	五月
June	*liùyuè*	六月
July	*qīyuè*	七月
August	*bāyuè*	八月
September	*jiǔyuè*	九月
October	*shíyuè*	十月
November	*shíyīyuè*	十一月
December	*shíèryuè*	十二月

Dates   日期

Dates start with the year, followed by the month and finally the day of the month. Thus, in Chinese, '1 January 1991' is literally 'one nine nine one, January, 1st'.

The following gives some examples of dates in Chinese, but you'll need to refer to the Numbers & Amounts, page 124, to work out the date for a particular day. The system is easy: for the year, say the number followed by *nián*; for the month, the number (January = one, September = nine, etc) followed by *yuè*; and for the day, the number followed by *hào*.

What date is it today?
  jīntiān jǐhào?   今天几号？
It's 28 June.
  liù yuè èrshíbā hào   六月二十八号
  (lit 'six month 28th')
It's 6 October.
  shí yuè liù hào   十月六号
  (lit '10 month 6th')

Present

today	*jīntiān*	今天
this morning	*jīntiān zǎoshang*	今天早上
this afternoon	*jīntiān xiàwǔ*	今天下午
tonight	*jīntiān wǎnshang*	今天晚上
this week	*zhèige xīngqī*	这个星期
this month	*zhèige yuè*	这个月
this year	*jīnnián*	今年
immediately	*mǎshàng*	马上
now	*xiànzài*	现在

Past

yesterday	*zuótiān*	昨天
day before yesterday	*qiántiān*	前天
yesterday morning	*zuótiān zǎoshang*	昨天早上
yesterday afternoon	*zuótiān xiàwǔ*	昨天下午
last night/evening	*zuótiān wǎnshang*	昨天晚上
last week	*shàngge xīngqī*	上个星期
last month	*shàngge yuè*	上个月
last year	*qùnián*	去年

Future

tomorrow	*míngtiān*	明天
day after tomorrow	*hòutiān*	后天
tomorrow morning	*míngtiān zǎoshang*	明天早上
tomorrow afternoon	*míngtiān xiàwǔ*	明天下午
tomorrow evening/night	*míngtiān wǎnshang*	明天晚上
next week	*xiàge xīngqī*	下个星期
next month	*xiàge yuè*	下个月
next year	*míngnián*	明年

Some Useful Words 应用词句词汇

after	*yǐhòu*	以后
always	*zǒngshi*	总是
before	*yǐqián*	以前
century	*shìjì*	世纪
day	*rì*	日

early	*zǎo*	早
every day	*měitiān*	每天
forever	*yǒngyuǎn*	永远
midnight	*wǔyè*	午夜
month	*yuè*	月
never	*cónglái méi ...*	从来没...
night	*yè*	夜
noon	*zhōngwǔ*	中午
recently	*zuìjìn*	最近
sunrise	*rìchū*	日出
sunset	*rìluò*	日落

Seasons 传统节日

summer	*xiàtiān*	夏天
autumn	*qiūtiān*	秋天
winter	*dōngtiān*	冬天
spring	*chūntiān*	春天

Festivals & Holidays 中国历朝

Days off are something of a rarity for the Chinese. Consequently festivals and public holidays are celebrated enthusiastically. Most of the big festivals are calculated according to the lunar calendar and fall on different dates every year.

chūnjié 春节

Also known as the Spring Festival, this is Chinese New Year, held in late January or early February, and a big family celebration lasting several days.

yuánxiāojié 元宵节

Held shortly after the Spring Festival, it marks the formal end of the New Year celebrations with fire crackers and special *yuánxiāo* sweets.

qīngmíngjié 清明节

Also known as 'Clear & Bright', this is a time when people traditionally go to sweep and tidy up the tombs of their ancestors; held in April.

dūanwǔjié 端午节

Known in English as the Dragon Boat Festival, *dūanwǔjié* takes place in late May/early June, and commemorates the death by drowning of a virtuous poet/official in the 4th century BC.

zhōngqiūjié 中秋节

Known as the Moon Festival, people get together at full moon in late September/early October to 'moon-watch' and eat moon-shaped sweet cakes.

Chinese Dynasties

In China historical time is marked by dynasties. When you go sightseeing you are likely to come across references to them.

xià	2100-1600 BC	夏
shāng	1600-1100 BC	商
xīzhōu Western Zhou	1100-771 BC	西周
chūnqiū Spring & Autumn Period	770-476 BC	春秋
zhànguó Warring States Period	475-221 BC	战国
qín	221-207 BC	秦
xīhàn Western Han	206 BC-24 AD	西汉
dōnghàn Eastern Han	25-220	东汉
sānguó Three Kingdoms Period	220 -265	三国
xījìn Western Jin	265-316	西晋
dōngjìn Eastern Jin	317-420	东晋
nánběicháo Southern & Northern Dynasties Period	420-582	南北朝
suí	581-618	隋
táng	618-907	唐
wǔdài Five Dynasties Period	907-960	五代
liáo	916-1125	辽

sòng	960-1279	宋
jīn	1125-1234	金
yuán	1271-1368	元
míng	1368-1644	明
qīng	1644-1911	清

Numbers & Amounts

数字

The counting system in Chinese is very easty to learn. Multiples of 10 are made by stating the multiple and then 10 – so 20 is literally 'two ten'. If you learn the numbers from one to 10 you can count to 100 without having to learn any new vocabulary. The only exception is the number two; when counting, two is *èr* and when used with measure words (see Measure Words in Grammar, page 18) it is *liǎng*.

Cardinal Numbers

字 数

0	*líng*	零
1	*yī*	一
2	*èr*	二
3	*sān*	三
4	*sì*	四
5	*wǔ*	五
6	*liù*	六
7	*qī*	七
8	*bā*	八
9	*jiǔ*	九
10	*shí*	十
11	*shíyī*	十一
12	*shíèr*	十二
13	*shísān*	十三

14	*shísì*	十四
15	*shíwǔ*	十五
16	*shíliù*	十六
17	*shíqī*	十七
18	*shíbā*	十八
19	*shíjiǔ*	十九
20	*èrshí*	二十
21	*èrshíyī*	二十一
22	*èrshíèr*	二十二
23	*èrshísān*	二十三
30	*sānshí*	三十
31	*sānshíyì*	三十一
40	*sìshí*	四十
50	*wǔshí*	五十
60	*liùshí*	六十
70	*qīshí*	七十
80	*bāshí*	八十
90	*jiǔshí*	九十
100	*yìbǎi*	一百
101	*yìbǎilíngyī*	一百零一
102	*yìbǎilíngèr*	一百零二
110	*yìbǎiyìshí*	一百一十
189	*yìbǎibāshíjiǔ*	一百八十九
200	*liǎngbǎi/èrbǎi*	两百/二百
300	*sānbǎi*	三百
1000	*yìqiān*	一千
10,000	*yíwàn*	一万
100,000	*shíwàn*	十万
1 million	*yìbǎiwàn*	一百万
100 million	*yíyì*	一亿

Ordinal Numbers 分数

Simply prefix any number with *dì* and it becomes an ordinal.

1st	*dìyī*	第一
2nd	*dìèr*	第二
3rd	*dìsān*	第三
10th	*dìshí*	第十

Fractions 数序

⅓	*sānfēnzhīyī*	三分之一
¼	*sìfēnzhīyī*	四分之一
½	*yíbàn*	一半
¾	*sìfēnzhīsān*	四分之三

Some Useful Words 应用词汇

once	*yícì*	一次
twice	*liǎngcì*	两次
three times	*sāncì*	三次
double	*liǎngbèi*	两倍
triple	*sānbèi*	三倍
about	*zuǒyòu*	左右
to count	*jìshù*	计算
a dozen	*yìdá*	一打
Enough!	*gòule!*	够了!
How much/many?	*dūoshǎo?*	多少
a little (amount)	*yìdiǎnrdiǎnr*	一点儿点儿
few	*shǎo*	少
many/a lot	*hěn dūo*	很多
too much	*tài dūole*	太多了
a pair	*yìshūang*	一双

NUMBERS & AMOUNTS

Vocabulary

词汇

A

abacus	*suànpan*	算盘
abdomen	*fùbù*	腹部
abortion	*liúchǎn*	流产
about	*dàyūe*	大约
above	*shàng*	上
accept	*shōu*	收
accident	*shìgù*	事故
ache	*téng*	疼
actor	*yǎnyuán*	演员
acupuncture	*zhēnjiǔ*	针灸
adaptor	*chāzuò*	插座
address	*dìzhǐ*	地址
address book	*tōngxùnbù*	通讯簿
admire	*zànshǎng*	赞赏
admission	*rùchǎng*	入场
adventure	*màoxiǎn*	冒险
aeroplane	*fēijī*	飞机
afraid	*pà*	怕
afternoon	*xiàwǔ*	下午
after(wards)	*yǐhòu*	以后
again	*zài*	再
against	*duì*	对
age	*niánlíng*	年龄
ago	*qián*	前
agree	*tóngyì*	同意
agriculture	*nóngyè*	农业

air	*kōngqì*	空气
air-conditioned	*kōngtiáo*	空调
air pollution	*kōngqìwūrǎn*	空气污染
airmail	*hángkōng*	航空
airport	*fēijīchǎng*	飞机场
alarm clock	*nàozhōng*	闹钟
alcohol	*jiǔ*	酒
all	*dōu*	都
allergic	*guòmín*	过敏
also	*yě*	也
alter	*gǎi*	改
ambassador	*dàshǐ*	大使
ancient	*gǔdàide*	古代的
and	*hé*	和
angry	*shēngqì*	生气
animal	*dòngwu*	动物
ankle	*jiǎohuái*	脚踝
answer	*huídá*	回答
ant	*mǎyǐ*	蚂蚁
antibiotics	*kàngshēngsù*	抗生素
antique	*gǔwán*	古玩
antiseptic cream	*fǎngfǔjì*	防腐剂
appendicitis	*lánwěiyán*	烂尾炎
apple	*píngguǒ*	苹果
appointment	*yūehuì*	约会
approximately	*dàyūe*	大约
apricot	*xìng*	杏
archaeology	*kǎogǔxué*	考古学
architecture	*jiànzhùxué*	建筑学
argue	*chǎojià*	吵架
arm	*gēbo*	胳膊

arrive	dào	到
art	yìshù	艺术
artist	yìshùjiā	艺术家
arts & crafts	gōngyì měishù	工艺美术
ashtray	yānhuīgāng	烟灰缸
ask	wèn	问
aspirin	āsīpǐlín	阿司匹林
asthma	xiàochuǎn	哮喘
at	zài	在
automatic	zìdòngde	自动的
autumn	qiūtiān	秋天

B

baby	yīngér	婴儿
baby food	yīngér shípǐn	婴儿食品
babysitter	línshí bǎomǔ	临时保姆
back (body)	bèi	背
back (rear)	hòubian	后边
backpack	bèibāo	背包
bad	huài	坏
bag	dàizi	袋子
baggage	xíngli	行李
balcony	yángtái	阳台
ball	qiú	球
ballpoint	yuánzhūbǐ	圆珠笔
bamboo	zhúzi	竹子
banana	xiāngjiāo	香蕉
bandage	bēngdài	绷带
Band Aid	chuàngkětiē	创可贴
bank	yínháng	银行
banknote	chāopiào	

banknote	*chāopiào*	钞票
banquet	*yànhuì*	宴会
bar	*jiǔbā*	酒吧
barber's	*lǐfàdiàn*	理发店
bath	*yùgāng*	浴缸
bathing suit	*yǒuyǒngyī*	游泳衣
bathroom	*yùshì*	浴室
batteries	*diànchí*	电池
beach	*hǎitān*	海滩
beancurd	*dòufu*	豆腐
beans	*dòu*	豆
beard	*húzi*	胡子
beautiful	*piàoliang*	漂亮
because	*yīnwei*	因为
bed	*chuáng*	床
bedbugs	*chòuchóng*	臭虫
beef	*niúròu*	牛肉
beer	*píjiǔ*	啤酒
before	*yǐqián*	以前
beggar	*qǐgài*	乞丐
begin	*kāishǐ*	开始
behind	*zài ...hòumian*	在...后面
bell	*líng*	铃
below	*zài ...xiàmian*	在...下面
beside	*zài ...pángbian*	在...旁边
best	*zuì hǎo*	最好
better	*bǐjiào hǎo*	比较好
bicycle	*zìxíngchē*	自行车
big	*dà*	大
bill	*zhàngdān*	帐单
bird	*niǎo*	鸟

birthday	*shēngrì*	生日
biscuit	*bǐnggān*	饼干
bitter	*kǔde*	苦的
bladder	*pángguāng*	膀胱
blanket	*tǎnzi*	毯子
bleed	*liúxuě*	流血
blister	*shuǐpào*	水疱
blood	*xuě*	血
blood pressure	*xuěyā*	血压
blood transfusion	*shūxuě*	输血
blouse	*nǚchènshān*	女衬衫
blue	*lánsè*	蓝色
boat	*chuán*	船
body	*shēntǐ*	身体
boiled water	*kāishuǐ*	开水
bomb	*zhàdàn*	炸弹
bone	*gǔtou*	骨头
book	*shū*	书
bookshop	*shūdiàn*	书店
boots	*xuēzi*	靴子
bored/boring	*mèn*	闷
borrow	*jiè*	借
boss (n)	*lǎobǎn*	老板
botanical gardens	*zhíwùyuǎn*	植物园
botany	*zhíwùxué*	植物学
bottle	*píng*	瓶
bottle opener	*kāipíngqì*	开瓶器
bowel	*dàcháng*	大肠
bowl	*wǎn*	碗
box	*hézi*	盒子
boy	*nánháir*	男孩儿

boyfriend	*nán péngyou*	男朋友
bra	*rǔzhào*	乳罩
bracelet	*shǒuzhuó*	手镯
brain	*nǎozi*	脑子
bread	*miànbāo*	面包
break	*nòng huài*	弄坏
breakfast	*zǎofàn*	早饭
breast	*rǔfáng*	乳房
breathe	*hūxī*	呼吸
bridge	*qiáo*	桥
bright	*míngliàng*	明亮
bring	*ná*	拿
broken	*huàile*	坏了
brooch	*xiōngzhēn*	胸针
brother	*xiōngdì*	兄弟
(older)	*gēge*	哥哥
(younger)	*dìdi*	弟弟
brothel	*jìyuàn*	妓院
brown	*hèsè*	褐色
bruise	*qīngzhǒng*	青肿
brush	*shuāzi*	刷子
bucket	*shuǐtǒng*	水桶
Buddhism	*fójiào*	佛教
bug	*chòuchóng*	臭虫
building/	*jiànzhù*	建筑
construction		
bulb	*diàndēngpào*	电灯泡
bull	*gōngniú*	公牛
burn (n)	*shāoshāng*	烧伤
bus	*gōnggòngqìchē*	公共汽车
bus stop	*qìchēzhàn*	汽车站

business	*shāngyè*	商业
businessperson	*shāngrén*	商人
busy	*máng*	忙
but	*dànshi*	但是
butter	*huángyóu*	黄油
buy	*mǎi*	买

C

cabin	*kècāng*	客舱
cake	*dàngāo*	蛋糕
cake shop	*gāodiǎndiàn*	糕点店
call (phone)	*dǎ diànhuà*	打电话
call (name)	*jiào*	叫
calligraphy	*shūfǎ*	书法
camel	*luòtuo*	骆驼
camera	*zhàoxiàngjī*	照相机
camp	*yěyíng*	野营
can (container)	*guàntou*	罐头
can/cannot	*néng/bùnéng*	能/不能
canal	*yùnhé*	运河
cancel	*qǔxiāo*	取消
cancer	*áizhèng*	癌症
candle	*làzhú*	蜡烛
cap (hat)	*màozi*	帽子
capital	*shǒudū*	首都
capitalism	*zīběnzhǔyì*	资本主义
car	*chē*	车
card (name)	*míngpiàn*	名片
carpet	*dìtǎn*	地毯
carrot	*húluóbo*	胡萝卜
carry	*tí/ná*	提/拿

VOCABULARY

cash (n)	*xiànjīn*	现金
cassette	*héshìcídài*	盒式磁带
cat	*māo*	猫
Catholic	*tiānzhǔjiào*	天主教
cave	*shāndòng*	山洞
cemetery	*mùdì*	墓地
centre	*zhōngxīn*	中心
century	*shìjì*	世纪
ceramics	*táoqì*	陶器
certain	*quèdìng*	确定
chair	*yǐzi*	椅子
chance	*jīhuì*	机会
change (money – v)	*duìhuàn*	兑换
change (money – n)	*língqián*	零钱
cheap	*piányì*	便宜
Cheers!	*gānbēi!*	奶酪
cheese	*nǎilào*	乳酪
chemist (pharmacy)	*yàodiàn*	药店
chemistry	*huàxué*	化学
cheque	*zhīpiào*	支票
chicken	*jī*	鸡
child	*háizi*	孩子
chilli	*làjiāo*	辣椒
chocolate	*qiǎokèlì*	巧克力
chop (for name)	*yìnzhāng*	印章
chopsticks	*kuàizi*	筷子
choose	*tiāoxuǎn*	挑选
Christmas	*shèngdànjié*	圣诞节
church	*jiàotáng*	教堂
cigarettes	*xiāngyān*	香烟

city	chéngshì	城市
clean	gānjìng	干净
clock	zhōng	钟
closed (shop, etc)	guānmén	关门
clothing	yīfu	衣服
cloud	yún	云
coach (bus)	chángtúqìchē	长途汽车
coat	dàyī	大衣
coat hanger	guàyījià	挂衣架
cockroach	zhāngláng	蟑螂
coconut	yēziguǒ	椰子果
coffee	kāfēi	咖啡
cold	lěng	冷
colour	yánsè	颜色
comb	shūzi	梳子
come (v)	lái	来
comedy	xǐjù	喜剧
comfortable	shūfu	舒服
commune	gōngshè	公社
company (business)	gōngsī	公司
complex	fùzá	复杂
computer	diànnǎo	电脑
comrade	tóngzhì	同志
concert	yīnyuèhuì	音乐会
condom	bìyùntào	避孕套
conductor	shòupiàoyuán	售票员
confectionary	gāodiǎn	糕点
Congratulations!	gōngxǐ!	恭喜
constipation	biànmì	便秘
consulate	lǐngshìguǎn	领事馆

VOCABULARY

contact lens	*jiǎomó jiēchùjìng*	角膜接触镜
contagious	*chuánrǎn*	传染
contraceptive	*bìyùnyào*	避孕药
contract	*hétong*	合同
conversation	*huìhuà*	会话
copper	*tóng*	铜
coral	*shānhú*	珊瑚
corner	*jiǎo*	角
corner (street)	*lùkǒu*	路口
correct	*duì*	对
corrupt	*fǔbài*	腐败
cot	*xiǎo chuáng*	小床
cotton	*miánbù*	棉布
cotton wool	*tūozhǐmián*	脱脂棉
cough	*késou*	咳嗽
cough drops	*késou táng*	咳嗽糖
count (n)	*shùzì*	数字
count (v)	*jìsuàn*	计算
country (nation)	*guójiā*	国家
countryside	*nóngcūn/xiāngxià*	农村/乡下
court	*fǎyuàn*	法院
cow	*niú*	牛
crab	*pángxiè*	螃蟹
cramps	*chōujīn*	抽筋
crazy	*shénjīngbìng*	神经病
cream	*nǎiyóu*	奶油
credit card	*xìnyòngkǎ*	信用卡
crossroads	*shízìlùkǒu*	十字路口
cup/glass	*bēizi*	杯子
curtain	*chuānglián*	窗帘
customs	*hǎiguān*	海关

D

dad	bàba	爸爸
daily	rìchángde	日常的
damp	cháoshīde	潮湿的
dangerous	wēixiǎn	危险
dark	ànde	暗的
date	rìqī	日期
daughter	nǚér	女儿
dawn	límíng	黎明
day	tiān	天
dead	sǐde	死的
deaf	lóngde	聋的
decide/decision	juédìng	决定
deep	shēn	深
delay	yánhuǎn	延缓
delicious	hǎochī	好吃
delirious	shénzhìhūnmíde	神智昏迷的
deliver	sòng	送
democracy	mínzhǔ	民主
demonstration	shìwēi	示威
dentist	yáyī	牙医
denture	jiǎyá	假牙
deny	jùjué	拒绝
deodorant	chútǐxiùyè	除体臭液
department store	bǎihuò shāngdiàn	百货商店
departure	chūfā	出发
deposit	yājīn	押金
desert	shāmò	沙漠
dessert	tiánpǐn	甜品
destroy	pòhuài	破坏
diabetes	tángniàobìng	糖尿病

diaper (nappy)	*zhǐniàobù*	纸尿布
diarrhoea	*fùxiè*	腹泻
dictionary	*zìdiǎn*	字典
different	*bùyíyàng*	不一样
difficult	*nán*	难
dining car	*cānchē*	餐车
dining room	*cāntīng*	餐厅
dinner	*wǎnfàn*	晚饭
direction	*fāngxiàng*	方向
dirty	*zāng*	脏
disabled	*cánfèirén*	残废人
disco	*dísīkē*	迪斯科
discount	*zhékòu*	折扣
disinfectant	*xiāodújì*	消毒剂
dislocate	*tuōjiù*	脱臼
dissatisfied	*bùmǎnyì*	不满意
disturb	*dǎrǎo*	打扰
dizzy	*tóuyūn*	头晕
dock	*mǎtou*	码头
doctor	*dàifu/yīshēng*	大夫/医生
dog	*gǒu*	狗
doll	*wáwa*	娃娃
dollar	*yuán*	元
door	*mén*	门
dope	*dàmá*	大麻
dormitory	*sùshè*	宿舍
double bed	*shuāngrén chuáng*	双人床
double room	*shuāngrénfáng*	双人房
downstairs	*lóuxià*	楼下
downtown	*shìzhōngxīn*	市中心
dozen	*dá*	打

drawing pin	*túdīng*	图钉
dream	*mèng*	梦
dress	*nǚ\v fú*	女服
drink (n)	*yǐnliào*	饮料
drink (v)	*hē*	喝
drive (car)	*kāi (chē)*	开（车）
driver	*sījī*	司机
drug	*dúpǐn*	毒品
drunk	*zuì*	醉
dry	*gān*	干
dry cleaner's	*gānxǐdiàn*	干洗店
duck	*yā*	鸭
dumplings	*jiǎozi*	饺子
during	*zài ...de shíhou*	在...的时候
dust	*huīchén*	灰尘
duty (customs)	*shuì*	税

E

each	*měi*	每
ear	*ěrduo*	耳朵
earache	*ěrduo téng*	耳朵疼
early	*zǎo*	早
earn	*zhuàn*	赚
earring	*ěrhuán*	耳环
earthquake	*dìzhèn*	地震
east	*dōng*	东
easy	*róngyì*	容易
eat	*chī*	吃
economy	*jīngjì*	经济
education	*jiàoyù*	教育
eel	*mànyú*	鳗鱼

egg	*jīdàn*	鸡蛋
eggplant	*qiézi*	茄子
eight	*bā*	八
eighteen	*shíbā*	十八
eighty	*bāshí*	八十
elastic bandage	*tánxìngbēngdài*	弹性绷带
elbow	*zhǒu*	肘
election	*xuǎnjǔ*	选举
electricity	*diàn*	电
electric fan	*diànfēngshàn*	电风扇
elevator	*diàntī*	电梯
eleven	*shíyī*	十一
embarassed	*bùhǎoyìsi*	不好意思
embassy	*dàshǐguǎn*	大使馆
embroidery	*cìxiù*	刺绣
emergency	*jǐnjí qíngkuàng*	紧急情况
empty	*kōngde*	空的
engineer	*gōngchéngshī*	工程师
England	*yīngguó*	英国
enough	*zúgòu*	足够
entrance	*rùkǒu*	入口
envelope	*xìnfēng*	信封
equal (n)	*píngděng*	平等
equator	*chìdào*	赤道
Europe	*ōuzhōu*	欧洲
evening	*wǎnshang*	晚上
event	*shìjiàn*	事件
every	*měi*	每
exchange (v)	*huàn*	换
exchange rate	*duìhuànlǜ*	兑换率
excuse me	*duìbuqǐ*	对不起

exhausted	*lèihuàile*	累坏了
exhibition	*zhǎnlǎnhuì*	展览会
exit	*chūkǒu*	出口
expensive	*guì*	贵
experience	*jīngyàn*	经验
export	*chūkǒu*	出口
express (letter)	*kuàidì*	快递
express (train)	*tèkuài*	特快
extension cord	*jiēcháng diànxiàn*	接长电线
eye	*yǎnjīng*	眼睛
eye drops	*yǎnyàoshuǐ*	眼药水

F

face	*liǎn*	脸
factory	*gōngchǎng*	工厂
faint	*tóuhūn*	头昏
fall	*shuāidǎo*	摔倒
false	*jiǎde*	假的
family	*jiā*	家
fan	*shànzi*	扇子
far	*yuǎn*	远
fare	*piàojià*	票价
farm	*nóngchǎng*	农场
fast	*kuài*	快
fat	*pàng*	胖
father	*fùqin*	父亲
faucet	*shuǐlóngtóu*	水龙头
fault	*cuò*	错
fee	*fèi*	费
feel	*juéde*	觉得
ferry	*dùchuán*	渡船

fever	fāshāo	发烧
few	shǎo	少
field	tiándì	田地
fill in (form)	tiánxiě	填写
film (cinema)	diànyǐng	电影
film (photographic)	jiāojuǎn	胶卷
find	zhǎo	找
fine (penalty)	fákuǎn	罚款
finger	shǒuzhǐ	手指
fire	huǒzāi	火灾
first	dìyī	第一
first aid kit	jíjiùxiāng	急救箱
first class	tóuděng	头等
fish	yú	鱼
fizzy drink	qìshuǐ	汽水
flag	qí	旗
flash (camera)	shǎnguāngdēng	闪光灯
flat	píng	平
flea	zǎo	蚤
flight	hángbān	航班
flood	shuǐzāi	水灾
flour	miànfěn	面粉
flower	huā	花
flu	gǎnmào	感冒
fly	fēi	飞
fog	wù	雾
folk music	mínjiānyīnyuè	民间音乐
follow	gēnsuí	跟随
food	shíwù	食物
food poisoning	shíwùzhòngdú	食物中毒

foot	jiǎo	脚
football (soccer)	zúqiú	足球
forest	sēnlín	森林
forget	wàngji	忘记
forgive	yuánliàng	原谅
fork	chāzi	叉子
form	biǎo	表
fountain	quán	泉
France	fǎguó	法国
free (cost)	miǎnfèi	免费
free (time)	yǒu kòng	有空
free (vacant)	méirén	没人
free market	zìyóushìchǎng	自由市场
French	fǎyǔ	法语
fresh	xīnxiān	新鲜
friend	péngyou	朋友
friendly	yǒuhǎo	友好
friendship store	yǒuyìshāngdiàn	友谊商店
from	cóng	从
fruit	shuǐguǒ	水果
fruit juice	guǒzhī	果汁
full	mǎn	满
funny	hǎoxiào	好笑
furniture	jiājù	家具

G

game	yóuxì	游戏
garbage	lājī	垃圾
garden	huāyuán	花园
garlic	suàn	蒜
gas	méiqì	煤气

gate	*mén*	门
gauze	*shābù*	纱布
genuine	*zhēnde*	真的
geology	*dìzhìxué*	地质学
German (language)	*déyǔ*	德语
Germany	*déguó*	德国
gift	*lǐwù*	礼物
ginger	*jiāng*	姜
ginseng	*rénshēn*	人参
girl	*niǚ háizi*	女孩子
girlfriend	*niǚ péngyou*	女朋友
give	*gěi*	给
glass	*bēizi*	杯子
glasses (spectacles)	*yǎnjìng*	眼镜
glove	*shǒutào*	手套
glue	*jiāoshuǐ*	胶水
go	*qù*	去
gold	*jīn*	金
good	*hǎo*	好
goodbye	*zàijiàn*	再见
goods	*huòpǐn*	货品
goose	*é*	鹅
go out	*chūqu*	出去
government	*zhèngfu*	政府
gram	*kè*	克
grape	*pútáo*	葡萄
grass	*cǎo*	草
gray	*huīsè*	灰色
greasy	*yóuwūde*	油污的
green	*lǜsè*	绿色
green tea	*liǚ chá*	绿茶

grocery	fùshídiàn	副食店
group	tuántǐ	团体
guide	dǎoyóu	导游
guidebook	lǚ͎v yóuzhǐnán	旅游指南
guitar	jítā	吉他
gymnastics	tǐcāo	体操
gynaecologist	fùkēyīshēng	妇科医生

H

hair	tóufa	头发
hairdressers	lǐfàdiàn	理发店
half	bàn	半
ham	huǒtuǐ	火腿
hand	shǒu	手
handbag	shǒutíbāo	手提包
handkerchief	shǒupà	手帕
handmade	shǒugōngzhìde	手工制的
handsome	yīngjùn	英俊
happy	gāoxìng	高兴
harbour	gǎngwān	港湾
hard (difficult)	nán	难
hard seat	yìngzuò	硬座
hard sleeper	yìngwò	硬卧
hate	hèn	恨
have	yǒu	有
he	tā	他
head	tóu	头
headache	tóuténg	头疼
health	jiànkāng	健康
hear	tīngjiàn	听见
heart	xīnzàng	心脏

heating	nuǎnqì	暖气
heavy	zhòng	重
help (v)	bāngmáng	帮忙
Help!	jiùmìng!	救命!
her	tāde	她的
here	zhèr	这儿
high	gāo	高
hike	túbùlǚxíng	徒步旅行
hill	xiǎoshān	小山
hire	zū	租
his	tāde	他的
history	lìshǐ	历史
hitchhike	dāchē	搭车
holiday	jiàqī	假期
home	jiā	家
homesick	xiǎngjiā	想家
homosexual	tóngxìngliàn	同性恋
honest	chéngshí	诚实
honey	fēngmì	蜂蜜
hope	xīwàng	希望
hors d'oeuvres	kāiwèicài	开胃菜
horse	mǎ	马
hospital	yīyuàn	医院
hot	rè	热
hotel	lǚguǎn	旅馆
hot water	rèshuǐ	热水
hour	xiǎoshí	小时
house	fángwū	房屋
how	zěnme	怎么
hundred	bǎi	百
hungry	è	饿

hurry	hěn jí	很急
hurt (adj)	téng	疼
husband	zhàngfu	丈夫

I

I	wǒ	我
ice	bīng	冰
ice cream	bīngqílín	冰淇淋
idea	zhǔyì	主意
idiot	báichī	白痴
if	rúguǒ	如果
ill	bìngle	病了
illegal	bùhéfǎde	不合法的
immediately	mǎshàng	马上
import	jìnkǒu	进口
important	zhòngyào	重要
impossible	bùkěnéngde	不可能的
include	bāokuò	包括
inconvenient	bùfāngbiàn	不方便
incorrect	búduì	不对
increase	zēngjiā	增加
indigestion	xiāohuàbùliáng	消化不良
individual	gètǐde	个体的
industry	gōngyè	工业
infected	gǎnrǎn	感染
infectious	chuánrǎn	传染
inflammation	fāyán	发炎
inflation	tōnghuò péngzhàng	通货膨账
informal	fēizhèngshide	非正式的
information office	wènxùnchù	问讯处
injection	zhùshè	注射

injured	*shòushāngle*	受伤了
ink	*mòshuǐ*	墨水
insect	*chóngzi*	虫子
insect repellent	*chúchóngjì*	除虫剂
inside	*lǐmian*	里面
insurance	*bǎoxiǎn*	保险
intelligent	*cōngming*	聪明
interested (to be)	*gǎn xìngqu*	感兴趣
interesting	*yǒuqù*	有趣
international	*guójì*	国际
introduce	*jièshào*	介绍
investment	*tóuzī*	投资
invite	*qǐng*	请
Ireland	*àiěrlán*	爱尔兰
island	*dǎo*	岛
Italy	*yìdàlì*	意大利
itch	*yǎng*	痒
ivory	*xiàngyá*	象牙

J

jacket	*duǎnshàngyī*	短上衣
jade	*yù*	玉
jail	*jiānyù*	监狱
jam	*guǒjiàng*	果酱
Japan	*rìběn*	日本
jar	*guànzi*	罐子
jasmine tea	*mòlìhūachá*	茉莉花茶
jazz	*juéshìyīnyuè*	爵士音乐
jeans	*niúzǎikù*	牛仔裤
jewellery	*zhūbǎo*	珠宝
journalist	*jìzhě*	记者

juice	*zhī*	汁
jump	*tiào*	跳
jumper/sweater	*máoyī*	毛衣
jungle	*cónglín*	丛林

K

key	*yàoshi*	钥匙
kidney	*shèn*	肾
kill	*shā*	杀
kilogram	*gōngjīn*	公斤
kilometre	*gōngli*	公里
kind (type)	*zhǒng*	种
kindergarten	*yòuéryuán*	幼儿院
kiss	*wěn*	吻
kitchen	*chúfáng*	厨房
kite	*fēngzheng*	风筝
knee	*xīgài*	膝盖
knife	*dāozi*	刀子
know (person)	*rènshi*	认识
know (something)	*zhīdào*	知道

L

lace	*gōuzhībùliào*	钩织布料
lacquerware	*qīqì*	漆器
lake	*hú*	湖
lamb (meat)	*yángròu*	羊肉
lamp	*diàndēng*	电灯
landscape	*fēngjǐng*	风景
landslide	*shānbēng*	山崩
language	*yǔyán*	语言
large	*dàde*	大的

last	*zuìhòude*	最后的
late	*wǎn*	晚
laugh	*xiào*	笑
laundry (place)	*xǐyīdiàn*	洗衣店
law	*fǎlǜ*	法律
lawyer	*lǜshī*	律师
laxative	*huǎnxièjì*	缓泻剂
lazy	*lǎnduò*	懒惰
leader	*lǐngdǎo*	领导
learn	*xué*	学
leather	*pígé*	皮革
leave	*zǒu*	走
leave (train/bus)	*kāichē*	开车
leech	*shuǐzhì*	水蛭
left (direction)	*zuǒbian*	左边
left-luggage office	*xíngli jìcúnchù*	行李寄存处
leg	*tuǐ*	腿
legal	*héfǎ*	合法
lemon	*níngméng*	柠檬
lend	*jiè*	借
lens (camera)	*jìngtóu*	镜头
lens (glasses)	*jìngpiàn*	镜片
lens cap	*jìngtóugài*	镜头盖
less	*shǎo yìdiǎnr*	少一点
letter	*xìn*	信
letterwriting paper	*xìnzhǐ*	信纸
library	*túshūguǎn*	图书馆
lid	*gài*	盖
life	*shēnghuó*	生活
lift (elevator)	*diàntī*	电梯
light (colour)	*qiǎn*	浅

light (electric)	*diàndēng*	电灯
light (weight)	*qīngde*	轻的
lighter	*dǎhuǒjī*	打火机
lightning	*shǎndiàn*	闪电
like (v)	*xǐhuan*	喜欢
lip	*zuǐchún*	嘴唇
lipstick	*kǒuhóng*	口红
listen	*tīng*	听
litre	*shēng*	升
little	*yìdiǎnr*	一点儿
liver	*gān*	肝
lobster	*lóngxiā*	龙虾
long	*cháng*	长
long-distance call	*chángtú diànhuà*	长途电话
look	*kàn*	看
lose	*diū*	丢
loud	*chǎo*	吵
love (v)	*ài*	爱
low	*dī*	低
luck	*yùnqì*	运气
luggage	*xíngli*	行李
lump (swelling)	*zhǒngkuài*	肿块
lunch	*zhōngfàn*	午饭
lung	*fèi*	肺
lychees	*lìzhī*	荔枝

M

machine	*jīqì*	机器
mad	*fāfēng*	发疯
magazine	*zázhì*	杂志
mahjong	*májiàng*	麻将

mail (v)	*jì*	寄
main	*zhǔyào*	主要
makeup	*huàzhuāng*	化妆
man	*nánrén*	男人
manager	*jīnglǐ*	经理
mango	*mángguǒ*	芒果
many	*hěn duō*	很多
map	*dìtú*	地图
marble	*dàlǐshí*	大理石
market	*shìchǎng*	市场
married	*yǐjīng jiéhūnde*	已经结婚的
massage	*ànmó*	按摩
matches	*huǒchái*	火柴
mattress	*chuángdiàn*	床垫
maybe	*yěxǔ*	也许
meal	*fàn*	饭
measure (v)	*liáng*	量
meat	*ròu*	肉
mechanic	*jìgōng*	技工
medicine	*yào*	药
meet	*jiànmiàn*	见面
melon	*guā*	瓜
memorial hall	*jìniànguǎn*	纪念馆
mend	*xiūlǐ*	修理
menu	*càidān*	菜单
message	*liúhuà*	留话
metal	*jīnshǔ*	金属
method	*fāngfǎ*	方法
metre	*mǐ*	米
midday	*zhōngwǔ*	中午
middle	*zhōngjiān*	中间

midnight	wǔyè	午夜
milk	niúnǎi	牛奶
million	bǎiwàn	百万
mineral water	kuàngquánshuǐ	矿泉水
mint	bòhe	薄荷
minute	fēnzhōng	分钟
mirror	jìngzi	镜子
Miss	xiǎojiě	小姐
miss (long for)	xiǎng	想
mist	bówù	薄雾
mistake	cuòwu	错误
modern	xiàndàide	现代的
money	qián	钱
monkey	hóuzi	猴子
monosodium glutimate	wèijīng	味精
month	yuè	月
monument	jìniànbēi	纪念碑
moon	yuèliang	月亮
more	dūo yìdiǎnr	多一点儿
morning	zǎoshang	早上
mother	mǔqin	母亲
motorbike	mótūochē	摩托车
mountain	shān	山
mouth	zuǐ	嘴
move (v)	dòng	动
movie	diànyǐng	电影
Mr	xiānsheng	先生
Mrs	tàitai	太太
mud	ní	泥
muscle	jīròu	肌肉

museum	*bówùguǎn*	博物馆
music	*yīnyuè*	音乐
musical instrument	*yuèqì*	乐器
Muslim	*qīngzhēn*	清真
must	*bìxū*	必须
mutton	*yángròu*	羊肉
my	*wǒde*	我的

N

nail (finger)	*zhījia*	指甲
nail clippers	*zhījiadāo*	指甲刀
name	*xìngmíng*	姓名
nappy	*niàobù*	尿布
nationality	*guójí*	国籍
natural	*zìránde*	自然的
nature	*zìránjiè*	自然界
near	*jìn*	近
necessary	*bìyàode*	必要的
neck	*bózi*	脖子
necklace	*xiàngliàn*	项链
needle	*zhēn*	针
negative (film)	*dǐpiàn*	底片
never	*cónglái méiyǒu*	从来没有
new	*xīn*	新
news	*xīnwén*	新闻
newspaper	*bàozhǐ*	报纸
next	*xià*	下
nice	*hǎo*	好
night	*yè*	夜
no	*bù*	不
noisy	*chǎo*	吵

noodles	*miàntiáo*	面条
normal	*zhèngchángde*	正常的
north	*běi*	北
nose	*bízi*	鼻子
notebook	*bǐjìběn*	笔记本
note paper	*xìnzhǐ*	信纸
novel	*xiǎoshūo*	小说
novelist	*xiǎoshūojiā*	小说家
now	*xiànzài*	现在
number	*hàomǎ*	号码
nurse	*hùshi*	护士

O

obvious	*míngxiǎn*	明显
occupation	*zhíyè*	职业
ocean	*hǎiyáng*	海洋
office	*bàngōngshì*	办公室
officer	*jūngūan*	军官
often	*chángcháng*	常常
oil	*yóu*	油
ointment	*yàogāo*	药膏
old (person)	*lǎo*	老
old (thing)	*jiù*	旧
on	*zài ...shàng*	在...上
once	*yícì*	一次
one	*yíge*	一个
one-way ticket	*dānchéng piào*	单程票
onion	*yángcōng*	洋葱
only	*zhǐ*	只
open (sign)	*yíngyèzhōng*	营业中
open (v & adj)	*kāimén*	开门

VOCABULARY

operation	*shǒushù*	手术
opinion	*yìjiàn*	意见
opium	*yāpiàn*	鸦片
opportunity	*jīhuì*	机会
opposite	*zài ...duìmian*	在...对面
or	*háishi*	还是
orange (colour)	*júhóngsède*	桔红色的
orange (fruit)	*júzi*	桔子
orange juice	*júzizhī*	桔子汁
order (meal)	*diǎn cài*	点菜
ordinary	*pǔtōngde*	普通的
organisation	*zǔzhī*	组织
other	*biéde*	别的
outside	*zài ...wàimian*	在...外面
overalls	*gōngzhuāngkù*	工装裤
overcoat	*dàyī*	大衣
overnight	*yíyè*	一夜
overseas	*guówài*	国外
owe	*qiàn*	欠
ox	*gōngniú*	公牛
oyster	*háo*	蚝

P

packet	*bāo*	包
paddy field	*dàotián*	稻田
padlock	*guàsuǒ*	挂锁
page	*yè*	页
pagoda	*bǎotǎ*	宝塔
painful	*hěn téng*	很疼
painter	*huàjiā*	画家
painting	*huà*	画

pair	*yìshuāng*	一双
palace	*gōngdiàn*	宫殿
palpitation	*xīnjì*	心悸
pan	*gūo*	锅
paper	*zhǐ*	纸
parallel	*píngxíngde*	平行的
parcel	*bāoguǒ*	包裹
parents	*fùmǔqin*	父母亲
park	*gōngyuán*	公园
party	*wǎnhuì*	晚会
passport	*hùzhào*	护照
passport number	*hùzhào hàomǎ*	护照号码
pastry	*gāodiǎn*	糕点
pastry shop	*gāodiǎndiàn*	糕点店
path	*xiǎolù*	小路
patient	*bìngrén*	病人
pavillion	*tíngzi*	亭子
pay (v)	*fùqián*	付钱
pea	*wāndòu*	豌豆
peace	*hépíng*	和平
peach	*táozi*	桃子
peanut	*hūashēng*	花生
pear	*lí*	梨
pearl	*zhēnzhū*	珍珠
pedestrian	*xíngrén*	行人
pen	*bǐ*	笔
pencil	*qiānbǐ*	铅笔
penicillin	*qīngméisù*	青霉素
penknife	*xiǎodāo*	小刀
people	*rén*	人
pepper	*hújiāo*	胡椒

percent	*bǎifēnzhī*	百分之
perfect	*wánměi*	完美
performance	*yǎnchū*	演出
permit	*xǔkězhèng*	许可证
person	*rén*	人
personal	*sīrénde*	私人的
personality	*gèxìng*	个性
perspire	*chūhàn*	出汗
pharmacy	*yàodiàn*	药店
photo	*zhàopiàn*	照片
photocopy	*fùyìn*	复印
photography	*shèyǐng*	摄影
piece	*kuài*	块
pig	*zhū*	猪
pill	*piàn*	片
pill (contraceptive)	*bìyùnyào*	避孕药
pillow	*zhěntou*	枕头
pillowcase	*zhěntào*	枕套
pineapple	*bōluó*	菠萝
pink	*fěnhóngsè*	粉红色
pipe	*yāndǒu*	烟斗
place	*dìfang*	地方
plane	*fēijī*	飞机
plant	*zhíwù*	植物
plate	*pánzi*	盘子
platform (station)	*zhàntái*	站台
play	*wánr*	玩儿
play (theatre)	*xìjù*	戏剧
please	*qǐng*	请
plug	*chātóu*	插头
plum	*lǐzi*	李子

pocket	*kǒudài*	口袋
poet	*shīrén*	诗人
poison	*dúpǐn*	毒品
police	*jǐngchá*	警察
police station	*gōngānjú*	公安局
politics	*zhèngzhì*	政治
pond	*chítáng*	池塘
pool (swimming)	*yóuyǒngchí*	游泳池
poor	*qióng*	穷
porcelain	*cíqì*	瓷器
pork	*zhūròu*	猪肉
port	*mǎtou*	码头
post (v)	*jì*	寄
postage	*yóufèi*	邮费
postage stamp	*yóupiào*	邮票
postcard	*míngxìnpiàn*	明信片
post office	*yóujú*	邮局
potato	*tǔdòu*	土豆
pottery	*táoqì*	陶器
practical	*shíjì*	实际
prawn	*xiā*	虾
prefer	*bǐjiào xǐhuan*	比较喜欢
pregnant	*huáiyùn*	怀孕
prepare	*zhǔnbèi*	准备
prescription	*yàofāng*	药方
present (gift)	*lǐwù*	礼物
president	*zǒngtǒng*	总统
pressure	*yālì*	压力
pretty	*piàoliang*	漂亮
price	*jiàqián*	价钱
priest	*jiàoshì*	教士

prison	jiānyù	监狱
private	sīrén	私人
probably	dàgài	大概
problem	wèntí	问题
processing (film)	chōngxǐ	冲洗
product	chǎnpǐn	产品
profession	zhíyè	职业
professional	zhuānyède	专业的
programme	jiémù	节目
promise	dāyìng	答应
pronunciation	fāyīn	发音
property	cáichǎn	财产
prostitute	jìnǚ	妓女
protect	bǎohù	保护
Protestant	xīnjiào	新教
province	shěng	省
prune	méizi	梅子
psychology	xīnlǐxué	心理学
pull	lā	拉
pure	chúnde	纯的
purple	zǐsè	紫色
pus	nóng	脓
push	tuī	推

Q

quality	zhìliàng	质量
quantity	shùliàng	数量
quarrel	chǎojià	吵架
quarter	sìfēnzhīyī	四分之一
question	wèntí	问题
queue	páiduì	排队

quick	*kuài*	快
quiet	*ānjìng*	安静
quilt	*bèizi*	被子

R

rabbit	*tùzi*	兔子
racism	*zhǒngzúpiānjiàn*	种族偏见
radio	*shōuyīnjī*	收音机
railway station	*huǒchēzhàn*	火车站
rain (v)	*xiàyǔ*	下雨
raincoat	*yǔyī*	雨衣
rape	*qiángjiān*	强奸
rare	*nándé*	难得
rash	*zhěnzi*	疹子
raspberry	*mùméi*	木莓
rat	*hàozi*	耗子
raw	*shēngde*	生的
razor	*tìdāo*	剃刀
razor blades	*tìdāo piàn*	剃刀片
read	*kànshū*	看书
ready	*hǎole*	好了
real	*zhēnde*	真的
really	*zhēnde*	真的
reason	*yuányīn*	原因
receipt	*shōujù*	收据
recent	*zuìjìn*	最近
reception desk	*fúwùtái*	服务台
recommend	*tuījiàn*	推荐
record (disk)	*chàngpiàn*	唱片
red	*hóngsè*	红色
refrigerator	*bīngxiāng*	冰箱

VOCABULARY

refugee	*nànmín*	难民
refund	*tuìkuǎn*	退款
refuse	*jùjué*	拒绝
region	*dìqū*	地区
registered (mail)	*guàhào*	挂号
relation(ship)	*gūanxi*	关系
religion	*zōngjiào*	宗教
remember	*jìde*	记得
rent/hire	*zū*	租
repair	*xiū*	修
report (v)	*bàogào*	报告
representative	*dàibiǎo*	代表
reptile	*páxíngdòngwu*	爬行动物
reserve/reservation	*yùdìng*	预定
responsibility	*zérèn*	责任
rest	*xiūxi*	休息
restaurant	*fànguǎn*	饭馆
return (give back)	*huán*	还
return (go back)	*huíqù*	回去
return (come back)	*huílái*	回来
return **ticket**	*láihúi piào*	来回票
reverse charges	*duìfāngfùfèi*	对方付费
revolution	*gémìng*	革命
rib	*lèigǔ*	肋骨
rice (uncooked)	*mǐ*	米
rice (cooked)	*báifàn*	白饭
right (side)	*yòubian*	右边
right (correct)	*duì*	对
ring (jewellery)	*jièzhi*	戒指
ripe	*chéngshóu*	成熟
river	*hé*	河

road	*lù*	路
rock	*yánshí*	岩石
roof	*wūdǐng*	屋顶
room	*fángjiān*	房间
room number	*fángjiān hàomǎ*	房间号码
round	*yuánde*	圆的
rubbish	*lājī*	垃圾
rug	*xiǎo dìtǎn*	小地毯
ruins	*jiùzhǐ*	旧址
run	*pǎobù*	跑步

S

sad	*bēiāide*	悲哀的
safe (n)	*bǎoxiǎnxiāng*	保险箱
safe (adj)	*ānquán*	安全
safety pin	*biézhēn*	别针
sailor	*shuǐshǒu*	水手
salt	*yán*	盐
same	*yíyàng*	一样
sandals	*liángxié*	凉鞋
sandwich	*sānmíngzhì*	三明治
sanitary towels	*wèishēngjīn*	卫生巾
satisfied	*mǎnyì*	满意
sausage	*xiāngcháng*	香肠
scald	*tàngshāng*	烫伤
scarf	*wéijīn*	围巾
scenery	*fēngjǐng*	风景
school	*xuéxiào*	学校
scissors	*jiǎndāo*	剪刀
scrambled egg	*chǎojīdàn*	炒鸡蛋
screwdriver	*qǐzi*	起子

VOCABULARY

scroll	*juànzhóu*	卷轴
sea	*hǎi*	海
seafood	*hǎixiān*	海鲜
seasick	*yùnchuán*	晕船
season	*jìjié*	季节
seat	*zuòwei*	座位
second	*dièr*	第二
second (time)	*miǎo*	秒
second class	*èrděng*	二等
secret	*mìmì*	秘密
secretary	*mìshu*	秘书
see	*kàn*	看
see (meet)	*jiànmiàn*	见面
sell	*mài*	卖
send (post)	*jì*	寄
sentence (language)	*jùzi*	句子
serious	*yánsù*	严肃
serious (injury)	*yánzhòngde*	严重的
service	*fúwù*	服务
sew	*féng*	缝
shampoo	*xǐfàjì*	洗发剂
shape	*xíngzhuàng*	形状
shave	*guāliǎn*	刮脸
she	*tā*	她
sheep	*yáng*	羊
sheet	*bèidān*	被单
shell	*bèiké*	贝壳
ship	*chuán*	船
shirt	*chènshān*	衬衫
shoe	*xié*	鞋
shoe lace	*xiédài*	鞋带

shoe polish	*xiéyóu*	鞋油
shop	*shāngdiàn*	商店
shopping area	*shāngyèqū*	商业区
shore	*àn*	岸
short	*duǎn*	短
short (height)	*ǎi*	矮
shorts	*duǎnkù*	短裤
shoulder	*jiānbǎng*	肩膀
shower	*línyù*	淋浴
shrimp	*xiā*	虾
shut	*gūan*	关
shy	*hàixiū*	害羞
sick	*shēngbìng*	生病
side	*pángbiān*	旁边
sightseeing	*yóulǎn*	游览
signature	*qiānmíng*	签名
silk	*sīchóu*	丝绸
silk factory	*sīchóuchǎng*	丝绸厂
silver	*yín*	银
simple	*jiǎndān*	简单
since	*cóng*	从
sing	*chànggē*	唱歌
single (unmarried)	*dānshēn*	单身
single room	*dānrénfáng*	单人房
single ticket	*dānchéngpiào*	单程票
sister (older)	*jiějie*	姐姐
(younger)	*mèimei*	妹妹
sit	*zuò*	坐
situation	*qíngkuàng*	情况
size	*dàxiǎo*	大小
size (clothes)	*chǐcùn*	尺寸

skin	*pífu*	皮肤
skirt	*qúnzi*	裙子
sky	*tiānkōng*	天空
sleep	*shuìjiào*	睡觉
sleeping pill	*ānmiányào*	安眠药
sleepy	*kùn*	困
sleeve	*xiùzi*	袖子
slipper	*tūoxié*	拖鞋
slow	*màn*	慢
small	*xiǎo*	小
small change	*língqián*	零钱
smelly	*chòu*	臭
smile	*xiào*	笑
smoke (v)	*chōuyān*	抽烟
snack	*xiǎochī*	小吃
snake	*shé*	蛇
snow (v)	*xiàxuě*	下雪
soap	*féizào*	肥皂
soccer	*zúqiú*	足球
socialism	*shèhuìzhǔyì*	社会主义
sock	*wàzi*	袜子
soft	*ruǎn*	软
soft seat	*ruǎnzuò*	软座
soft sleeper	*ruǎnwò*	软卧
soil	*nítǔ*	泥土
some	*yìxiē*	一些
son	*érzi*	儿子
song	*gēqǔ*	歌曲
soon	*bùjiǔ*	不久
sorry	*duìbuqǐ*	对不起
soup	*tāng*	汤

south	*nán*	南
souvenir	*jìniànpǐn*	纪念品
soya sauce	*jiàngyóu*	酱油
speak (v)	*shuō*	说
special	*tèbié*	特别
spicy	*là*	辣
spider	*zhīzhū*	蜘蛛
spine	*jǐzhuī*	脊椎
spoon	*sháozi*	勺子
sport	*tǐyùyùndòng*	体育运动
sprain	*niǔshāng*	扭伤
spring (season)	*chūntiān*	春天
square (place)	*guǎngchǎng*	广场
squid	*yóuyú*	鱿鱼
stairs	*lóutī*	楼梯
stale	*bùxīnxiān*	不新鲜
stamp	*yóupiào*	邮票
star	*xīngxing*	星星
start	*kāishǐ*	开始
station	*zhàn*	站
stationery	*wénjù*	文具
statistics	*tǒngjì*	统计
statue	*diāoxiàng*	雕像
stay	*zhù*	住
steal	*tōu*	偷
steamed	*qīngzhēngde*	清蒸的
steamed bread	*mántou*	馒头
stick	*mùgùn*	木棍
stomach	*wèi*	胃
stop (v)	*tíng*	停
Stop!	*zhànzhù!*	站住!

store (shop)	*shāngdiàn*	商店
storm	*fēngbào*	风暴
storey	*lóu*	楼
story (narrative)	*gùshi*	故事
stove	*huǒlú*	火炉
straight ahead	*yìzhí*	一直
strange	*qíguài*	奇怪
stranger	*mòshēngrén*	陌生人
strawberry	*cǎoméi*	草莓
street	*jiē*	街
string	*shéngzi*	绳子
strong	*yǒulì*	有力
student	*xuésheng*	学生
study	*xué*	学
stupid	*bèn*	笨
sturdy	*jiēshi*	结实
subway	*dìtiě*	地铁
success	*chénggōng*	成功
sugar	*táng*	糖
suit	*yítào xīfú*	一套西服
suitcase	*xiāngzi*	箱子
suite	*tàofáng*	套房
summer	*xiàtiān*	夏天
sun	*tàiyang*	太阳
sunburn	*shàishāng*	晒伤
sunglasses	*mòjìng*	墨镜
sunrise	*rìchū*	日出
suntan cream	*shàihēigāo*	晒黑膏
supermarket	*chāojíshìchǎng*	超级市场
sure	*yídìng*	一定
surface mail	*pǔtōng*	普通

VOCABULARY

swamp	*zhǎozé*	沼泽
sweater	*máoyī*	毛衣
sweet	*tián*	甜
swim	*yóuyǒng*	游泳
swimming pool	*yóuyǒngchí*	游泳池
swimsuit	*yóuyǒngyī*	游泳衣
swollen	*zhǒngle*	肿了
system	*xìtǒng*	系统

T

table	*zhuōzi*	桌子
table tennis	*pīngpāngqiú*	乒乓球
tailor's	*cáifengdiàn*	裁缝店
takeaway	*dàizǒu*	带走
talcum powder	*shuǎngshēnfěn*	爽身粉
talk	*shuōhuà*	说话
tall	*gāo*	高
tangerine	*gānjú*	柑橘
Taoism	*dàojiào*	道教
tap	*shuǐlóngtóu*	水龙头
tape recorder	*cídài lùyīnjī*	磁带录音机
tasty	*hǎochī*	好吃
tax	*shuì*	税
taxi	*chūzūqìchē*	出租汽车
tea	*chá*	茶
teacher	*jiàoshī*	教师
tea cup	*chábēi*	茶杯
team	*duì*	队
tea pot	*cháhú*	茶壶
teaspoon	*tāngchí*	汤匙
telegram	*diànbào*	电报

telephone	*diànhuà*	电话
telephone directory	*diànhuàbù*	电话簿
telephoto lens	*wàngyuǎn jìngtóu*	望远镜头
television	*diànshìjī*	电视机
telex	*diànchuán*	电传
tell	*gàosu*	告诉
temperature	*wēndù*	温度
tennis	*wǎngqiú*	网球
tennis court	*wǎngqiúchǎng*	网球场
tetanus	*pòshāngfēng*	破伤风
thanks	*xièxie*	谢谢
that	*nèige*	那个
theatre	*jùchǎng*	剧场
there	*nàr*	那儿
thick	*hòu*	厚
thief	*zéi*	贼
thigh	*dàtuǐ*	大腿
thin (slim)	*shòu*	瘦
think	*kǎolǜ*	考虑
thirsty	*kěle*	渴了
this	*zhèige*	这个
thousand	*qiān*	千
thread	*xiàn*	线
throat	*sǎngzi*	嗓子
through	*jīngguò*	经过
thumb	*mǔzhǐ*	拇指
thunder	*léi*	雷
ticket	*piào*	票
ticket office	*shòupiàochù*	售票处
tide	*cháo*	潮
tight (clothes)	*jǐn*	紧

time	shíjiān	时间
timetable	shíkèbiǎo	时刻表
tin (can)	guàntou	罐头
tin opener	kāiguànqì	开罐器
tip (gratuity)	xiǎofèi	小费
tired	lèile	累了
tissue paper	miànzhǐ	面纸
toast	kǎomiànbāo	烤面包
today	jīntiān	今天
toe	jiǎozhǐ	脚趾
together	yìqǐ	一起
toilet	cèsuǒ	厕所
toilet paper	wèishēngzhǐ	卫生纸
tomato	xīhóngshì	西红柿
tomb	língmù	陵墓
tomorrow	míngtiān	明天
tongue	shétou	舌头
tonight	jīnwǎn	今晚
too	tài	太
tooth	yá	牙
toothbrush	yáshuā	牙刷
toothpaste	yágāo	牙膏
toothpick	yáqiān	牙签
top	dǐng	顶
torch (flashlight)	shǒudiàntǒng	手电筒
tour group	lǚxíngtuán	旅行团
tourist	lǚkè	旅客
towards	xiàng	向
towel	máojīn	毛巾
tower	tǎ	塔
town	shìzhèn	市镇

toy	*wánjù*	玩具
trade	*màoyì*	贸易
traffic	*jiāotōng*	交通
traffic light	*hónglǚdēng*	红绿灯
train	*huǒchē*	火车
tram	*diànchē*	电车
transfer (bank)	*zhuǎnzhàng*	转帐
translate	*fānyì*	翻译
translator	*fānyì*	翻译
travel	*lǚxíng*	旅行
travel agency	*lǚxíngshè*	旅行社
travellers' cheque	*lǚxíng zhīpiào*	旅行支票
travelling bag	*lǚxíng bāo*	旅行包
tree	*shù*	树
trousers	*chángkù*	长裤
truck	*kǎchē*	卡车
try	*shì*	试
turn (change direction)	*guǎiwān*	拐弯
turtle	*hǎiguī*	海龟
tweezers	*nièzi*	镊子
twice	*liǎngcì*	两次
typhus	*bānzhěnshānghán*	斑疹伤寒

U

ugly	*chóulòude*	丑陋的
ulcer	*kuìyáng*	溃疡
umbrella	*yǔsǎn*	雨伞
uncomfortable	*bùshūfu*	不舒服
under	*zài ...xiàmian*	在...下面

underground (subway)	*dìtiě*	地铁
understand	*dǒng*	懂
underwear	*nèiyī*	内衣
unemployed	*shīyède*	失业的
USA	*měiguó*	美国
university	*dàxué*	大学
until	*dào*	到
up	*shàng*	上
upstairs	*lóushàng*	楼上
urgent	*jǐnjí*	紧急
urine	*niào*	尿
use	*yòng*	用
useful	*yǒuyòng*	有用

V

vacancy	*kōngfángjiān*	空房间
vacant	*kōngde*	空的
vacuum flask	*bǎowēnpíng*	保温瓶
valley	*shāngǔ*	山谷
valuable	*guìzhòngde*	贵重的
value	*jiàqián*	价钱
vegetable	*shūcài*	蔬菜
vegetarian	*chīsùde*	吃素的
vein	*jìngmài*	静脉
venereal disease	*xìngbìng*	性病
very	*hěn*	很
video camera	*shèxiàngjī*	摄像机
village	*cūnzhuāng*	村庄
vinegar	*cù*	醋
visa	*qiānzhèng*	签证

visit	fǎngwèn	访问
vomit	ǒutù	呕吐
vote	tóupiào	投票
vulgar	cūsúde	粗俗的

W

waist	yāo	腰
wait	děng	等
waiter/waitress	fúwùyuán	服务员
waiting room	hòuchēshì	候车室
wage	gōngzī	工资
wake (v)	jiàoxǐng	叫醒
walk	zǒulù	走路
wall	qiáng	墙
wallet	qiánbāo	钱包
want (v)	yào	要
war	zhànzhēng	战争
warm	nuǎnhuo	暖和
wash	xǐ	洗
washing powder	xǐyīfěn	洗衣粉
watch	biǎo	表
water	shuǐ	水
waterfall	pùbù	瀑布
watermelon	xīgūa	西瓜
wave	làng	浪
way (method)	fāngfǎ	方法
way (road)	lù	路
weak	ruò	弱
wealthy	yǒuqián	有钱
wear	chūan	穿
weather	tiānqi	天气

weather forecast	tiānqì yùbào	天气预报
wedding	hūnlǐ	婚礼
week	xīngqī	星期
weekend	zhōumò	周末
weigh	chēng	称
welcome	huānyíng	欢迎
well (n)	jǐng	井
well (health)	hěn hǎo	很好
west	xī	西
Western style	xīshì	西式
Westernised	xīhuàde	西化的
wet	shīde	湿的
what	shénme	什么
when	shénme shíhou	什么时候
where	nǎr	哪儿
which	něige	哪个
white	báisè	白色
who	shéi	谁
why	wèishénme	为什么
wide	kuān	宽
wife	qīzi	妻子
wildlife	yěshēngdòngwu	野生动物
win	yíng	赢
wind	fēng	风
window	chuānghu	窗户
wine	pútáojiǔ	葡萄酒
winter	dōngtiān	冬天
withdraw (bank)	qǔ	取
without	méiyǒu	没有
woman	nǚ rén	女人
wood	mùtóu	木头

wool	*chúnmáo*	纯毛
word	*cí*	词
work	*gōngzuò*	工作
world	*dìqiú*	地球
worse	*gèng huàile*	更坏了
worthwhile	*zhídé*	值得
wound	*shāngkǒu*	伤口
wrap	*bāo*	包
wrist	*shǒuwàn*	手腕
wristwatch	*shǒubiǎo*	手表
write	*xiě*	写
writer	*zuòjiā*	作家
writing paper	*xìnzhǐ*	信纸
wrong	*cuòde*	错的

X

| x-ray | *X gūangpiānzi* | X光片子 |

Y

year	*nián*	年
yellow	*huángsè*	黄色
yes	*duì*	对
yesterday	*zuótiān*	昨天
yoghurt	*sūannǎi*	酸奶
you	*nǐ*	你
young	*niánqīng*	年轻

Z

zero	*líng*	零
zoo	*dòngwùyuán*	动物园
zoology	*dòngwùxué*	动物学

Emergencies

紧急

Help!	*jiùmìng!*	救命!
Police!	*jǐngchá!*	警察!
Thief!	*xiǎotōu!*	小偷!
Watch out!	*xiǎoxīn diǎnr!*	小心点儿!
Go away!	*zǒu kāi!*	走开!

I've been robbed.
　　wǒ bèi dǎjiéle　　　　我被打劫了

I've been raped.
　　wǒ bèi qiángjiānle　　我被强奸了

There's been an accident!
　　chūshìle!　　　　　　出事了!

Call a doctor!
　　qǐng jiào yíwèi yīshēng!　请叫一位医生!

I am ill.
　　wǒ shēngbìngle　　　　我生病了

I am lost.
　　wǒ mílùle　　　　　　我迷路了

Where are the toilets?
　　cèsuǒ zài nǎr?　　　　厕所在哪儿?

They took my ...　*tāmen bǎ wǒde ...*　他们把我...偷走了
　　　　　　　　　tōuzǒule

I've lost my ...　*wǒ diūle wǒde ...*　我丢了我的...
　backpack　　　*bèibāo*　　　　　背包
　bag　　　　　*bāo*　　　　　　包
　camera　　　　*zhàoxiàngjī*　　照相机

177

money	*qían*	钱
passport	*hùzhào*	护照
watch	*shŏubiăo*	手表

I need ...	*wŏ xūyào ...*	我需要…
a doctor	*yīshēng*	医生
to go to a hospital	*qù yíge yīyuàn*	去一个医院

next of kin	*zuìjìnde qīnshŭ*	最近亲属

My blood group is (A, B, O, AB) positive/negative.
wŏde xuěxíng shi (A,B,O,AB) zhèng/fù

我的血型是 (A, B, O, AB)正/负

Could you help me please?
nĭ néngbunéng gĕi wŏ bānggemáng?

你能不能给我帮个忙?

I'm terribly sorry.
bàoqiàn, bàoqiàn

抱歉，抱歉

I didn't realise I was doing anything wrong.
wŏ bùzhīdào wŏ zuòcuòle shì

我不知道我作错了事

I didn't do it.
búshì wŏ zuòde

不是我作的

Could I please use the phone?
wŏ kĕyĭ dăge diànhuà ma?

我可以打个电话吗?

I wish to contact my embassy/consulate.
wŏ xiăng gēn wŏguóde dàshĭguăn/lĭánluò

我想跟我国的大使馆/领事馆联络

Index

179

LONELY PLANET PHRASEBOOKS

Complete your travel experience with a Lonely Planet phrasebook. Developed for the independent traveller, the phrasebooks enable you to communicate confidently in any practical situation – and get to know the local people and their culture.

Skipping lengthy details on where to get your drycleaning ironed, information in the phrasebooks covers bargaining, customs and protocol, how to address people and introduce yourself, explanations of local ways of telling the time, dealing with bureaucracy and bargaining, plus plenty of ways to share your interests and learn from locals.

Arabic (Egyptian)
Arabic (Moroccan)
Australian
*Introduction to Australian English,
Aboriginal and Torres Strait languages.*
Baltic States
*Covers Estonian, Latvian and
Lithuanian.*
Bengali
Brazilian
Burmese
Cantonese
Central Europe
*Covers Czech, French, German,
Hungarian, Italian and Slovak.*
Eastern Europe
*Covers Bulgarian, Czech, Hungarian,
Polish, Romanian and Slovak.*
Ethiopian (Amharic)
Fijian
French
German
Greek
Hindi/Urdu
Indonesian
Italian
Japanese
Korean
Lao
Latin American (Spanish)
Malay
Mandarin
Mongolian

Mediterranean Europe
*Covers Albanian, Greek, Italian,
Macedonian, Maltese, Serbian &
Croatian and Slovene.*
Nepali
Papua New Guinea (Pidgin)
Pilipino
Quechua
Russian
Scandinavian Europe
*Covers Danish, Finnish, Icelandic,
Norwegian and Swedish.*
South-East Asia
*Covers Burmese, Indonesian, Khmer,
Lao, Malay, Tagalog (Pilipino), Thai and
Vietnamese.*
Spanish
Sri Lanka
Swahili
Thai
Thai Hill Tribes
Tibetan
Turkish
Ukrainian
USA
*Introduction to US English,
Vernacular Talk, Native American
languages and Hawaiian.*
Vietnamese
Western Europe
*Useful words and phrases in Basque,
Catalan, Dutch, French, German, Irish,
Portuguese and Spanish (Castilian).*

COMPLETE LIST OF LONELY PLANET BOOKS

AFRICA
Africa - the South • Africa on a shoestring • Arabic (Moroccan) phrasebook • Cape Town • Central Africa • East Africa • Egypt • Egypt travel atlas • Ethiopian (Amharic) phrasebook • Kenya • Kenya travel atlas • Malawi, Mozambique & Zambia • Morocco • North Africa • South Africa, Lesotho & Swaziland • South Africa, Lesotho & Swaziland travel atlas • Swahili phrasebook • Trekking in East Africa• West Africa • Zimbabwe, Botswana & Namibia • Zimbabwe, Botswana & Namibia travel atlas
Travel Literature: The Rainbird: A Central African Journey • Songs to an African Sunset: A Zimbabwean Story

ANTARCTICA
Antarctica

AUSTRALIA & THE PACIFIC
Australia • Australian phrasebook • Bushwalking in Australia • Bushwalking in Papua New Guinea • Fiji • Fijian phrasebook • Islands of Australia's Great Barrier Reef • Melbourne • Micronesia • New Caledonia • New South Wales & the ACT • New Zealand • Northern Territory • Outback Australia • Papua New Guinea • Papua New Guinea phrasebook • Queensland • Rarotonga & the Cook Islands • Samoa • Solomon Islands • South Australia • Sydney • Tahiti & French Polynesia • Tasmania • Tonga • Tramping in New Zealand • Vanuatu • Victoria • Western Australia
Travel Literature: Islands in the Clouds • Sean & David's Long Drive

CENTRAL AMERICA & THE CARIBBEAN
Bermuda • Central America on a shoestring • Costa Rica • Cuba • Eastern Caribbean • Guatemala, Belize & Yucatán: La Ruta Maya • Jamaica

EUROPE
Amsterdam • Austria • Baltics States phrasebook • Britain • Central Europe on a shoestring • Central Europe phrasebook • Czech & Slovak Republics • Denmark • Dublin • Eastern Europe on a shoestring • Eastern Europe phrasebook • Estonia, Latvia & Lithuania • Finland • France • French phrasebook • German phrasebook • Greece • Greek phrasebook • Hungary • Iceland, Greenland & the Faroe Islands • Ireland • Italian phrasebook • Italy • Mediterranean Europe on a shoestring • Mediterranean Europe phrasebook • Paris • Poland • Portugal • Portugal travel atlas • Prague • Russia, Ukraine & Belarus • Russian phrasebook • Scandinavian & Baltic Europe on a shoestring • Scandinavian Europe phrasebook • Slovenia • Spain • Spanish phrasebook • St Petersburg • Switzerland • Trekking in Greece • Trekking in Spain • Ukrainian phrasebook • Vienna • Walking in Britain • Walking in Switzerland • Western Europe on a shoestring • Western Europe phrasebook
Travel Literature: The Olive Grove: Travels in Greece

INDIAN SUBCONTINENT
Bangladesh • Bengali phrasebook • Delhi • Hindi/Urdu phrasebook • India • India & Bangladesh travel atlas • Indian Himalaya • Karakoram Highway • Nepal • Nepali phrasebook • Pakistan • Rajasthan • Sri Lanka • Sri Lanka phrasebook • Trekking in the Indian Himalaya • Trekking in the Karakoram & Hindukush • Trekking in the Nepal Himalaya
Travel Literature: In Rajasthan • Shopping for Buddhas

COMPLETE LIST OF LONELY PLANET BOOKS

ISLANDS OF THE INDIAN OCEAN
Madagascar & Comoros • Maldives • Mauritius, Réunion & Seychelles

NORTH AMERICA
Alaska • Backpacking in Alaska • Baja California • California & Nevada • Canada • Florida • Hawaii • Honolulu • Los Angeles • Mexico • Miami • New England • New Orleans • New York, New Jersey & Pennsylvania • Pacific Northwest USA • Rocky Mountain States • San Francisco • Southwest USA • USA phrasebook • Washington, DC & the Capital Region

NORTH-EAST ASIA
Beijing • Cantonese phrasebook • China • Hong Kong • Hong Kong, Macau & Guangzhou • Japan • Japanese phrasebook • Japanese audio pack • Korea • Korean phrasebook • Mandarin phrasebook • Mongolia • Mongolian phrasebook • North-East Asia on a shoestring • Seoul • Taiwan • Tibet • Tibet phrasebook • Tokyo
Travel Literature: Lost Japan

MIDDLE EAST & CENTRAL ASIA
Arab Gulf States • Arabic (Egyptian) phrasebook • Central Asia • Iran • Israel & the Palestinian Territories • Israel & the Palestinian Territories travel atlas • Istanbul • Jerusalem • Jordan & Syria • Jordan, Syria & Lebanon travel atlas • Middle East • Turkey • Turkish phrasebook • Turkey travel atlas • Yemen
Travel Literature: The Gates of Damascus • Kingdom of the Film Stars: Journey into Jordan

SOUTH AMERICA
Argentina, Uruguay & Paraguay • Bolivia • Brazil • Brazilian phrasebook • Buenos Aires • Chile & Easter Island • Chile & Easter Island travel atlas • Colombia • Ecuador & the Galápagos Islands • Latin American Spanish phrasebook • Peru • Quechua phrasebook • Rio de Janeiro • South America on a shoestring • Trekking in the Patagonian Andes • Venezuela
Travel Literature: Full Circle: A South American Journey

SOUTH-EAST ASIA
Bali & Lombok • Bangkok • Burmese phrasebook • Cambodia • Ho Chi Minh City • Indonesia • Indonesian phrasebook • Indonesian audio pack • Jakarta • Java • Laos • Laos travel atlas • Lao phrasebook • Malay phrasebook • Malaysia, Singapore & Brunei • Myanmar (Burma) • Philippines • Pilipino phrasebook • Singapore • South-East Asia on a shoestring • South-East Asia phrasebook • Thailand • Thailand travel atlas • Thai phrasebook • Thai Hill Tribes phrasebook • Thai audio pack • Vietnam • Vietnamese phrasebook • Vietnam travel atlas

For ordering information contact your nearest Lonely Planet office.

PLANET TALK
Lonely Planet's FREE quarterly newsletter

Every issue is packed with up-to-date travel news and advice including:

- a letter from Lonely Planet co-founders Tony and Maureen Wheeler
- go behind the scenes on the road with a Lonely Planet author
- feature article on an important and topical travel issue
- a selection of recent letters from travellers
- details on forthcoming Lonely Planet promotions
- complete list of Lonely Planet products

To join our mailing list contact any Lonely Planet office.

LONELY PLANET PUBLICATIONS

AUSTRALIA
PO Box 617, Hawthorn 3122, Victoria
tel: (03) 9819 1877 fax: (03) 9819 6459
e-mail: talk2us@lonelyplanet.com.au

USA
150 Linden Street,
Oakland, CA 94607
tel: (510) 893 8555
TOLL FREE: 800 275-8555
fax: (510) 893 8572
e-mail: info@lonelyplanet.com

UK
10a Spring Place,
London NW5 3BH
tel: (0171) 428 4800 fax: (0171) 428 4828
e-mail: go@lonelyplanet.co.uk

FRANCE:
1 rue du Dahomey,
75011 Paris
tel: 01 55 25 33 00 fax: 01 55 25 33 01
e-mail: bip@lonelyplanet.fr

World Wide Web: http://www.lonelyplanet.com
or AOL keyword: lp